CITIZENSHIP
FOR YOU

Bhavini Algarra

Julie Easy

Don Harrison

Anne Hudson

Suzanne Erlewyn Lajeunesse

Peter Pattisson

Gillian Symons

Helen Young

General editor:
Lee Jerome

INSTITUTE FOR
CITIZENSHIP

Published in 2002 by:

Nelson Thornes Ltd
Delta Place
27 Bath Road
CHELTENHAM
GL53 7TH
United Kingdom

02 03 04 05 06 / 10 9 8 7 6 5 4 3 2 1

A catalogue record for this book is available from the British Library

ISBN 0 7487 6774 6

Edited by Katherine James
Picture research by Penni Bickle
Illustrations by Ian Foulis, Peter Lubach and Angela Lumley
Page make-up by Ann Samuel

Printed and bound in Spain by Graficas Estella

The Institute for Citizenship is an independent charitable trust that works to promote informed active citizenship and greater participation in democracy and society. It was established in 1992 by the then Speaker of the House of Commons, the Rt Hon. Bernard Weatherill, MP. The Institute develops and pilots innovative citizenship education resources, undertakes research and seeks to stimulate debate around citizenship issues. The work of the Institute for Citizenship is made possible through a wide range of local and national partnerships.
For further information visit: www.citizen.org.uk

Citizenship for You has been designed to meet the requirements of the Key Stage 4 Programme of Study for Citizenship and the specification requirements of Edexcel, OCR and AQA short courses in Citizenship Studies. It comprises the following elements:
- student textbook covering Citizenship skills and content
- on-line case studies, exploring Citizenship skills and knowledge through longer projects based on topical issues
- Teacher Support Pack containing photocopiable worksheets, additional activities and lesson notes to support the use of the student textbook.

Acknowledgements

With thanks to the following for permission to reproduce photographs and other copyright material in this book:

AFP: p 110 (top); Associated Press Ltd: cover (middle), pp 15 (top) (Springler), 88 (left) (Collins), 88 (right) (Baldwin), 90 (top) (Bouji), 90 (bottom) (Bandi), 91 (Azim), 106 (top) (AP Photo), 106 (bottom) (Vogel), 108 (top) (AP Photo), (middle) (Gur), 109 (Schadeburg) 110 (bottom) (Rousseau) 111 (top) (Melville) 111 (bottom) (Giles); Bridgeman Art Library: p 28 (top and bottom right and bottom left); Peter Brookes / Times Newspapers Ltd (30 May 2001): p 85; BTCV: p 112; Citizens Advice Bureau: p 112; Crime Concern: p 112; Everychild: p 103; Empics: p 41; Friends of the Earth: p 102; Sally and Richard Greenhill: pp 7, 24 (top and bottom right), 32 (all), 36, 44, 46 (both), 47, 68, 100, 117 (all); Groundwork: 112; Hulton Deutsch Collection: p 94; La Belle Aurore (Davey): pp 66, 70, 78; Maidstone & The Weald Conservative Association: p 60; Kenneth Mahood / Council for Education in World Citizenship: p 27; Panos Pictures: pp 15 (bottom) (Davies), 24 (middle right) (Hartley) (bottom right) (Sprague); Panos Publications: p 26; Plan International: p 103; Popperfoto: pp 28 (bottom middle) (Reuters/Christensen), 62 (top) (Waldie) (second from top) (Pool/Reuters) and (third row left) (Chung), (third row right) (Reuters/Hodgson), 87 (Reuters/Pool), 109 (United Press International), 120 (top) (Reuters/Garcia); PA Photos: cover (bottom), pp 62 (bottom), 79, 85,119; Project Trust: p 112; PYMCA: p 71 (Fisk); Rex Features: pp 62 (third row middle), 95; Report Digital: cover (top); Science Photo Library: p 104; Shout Pictures: p 8; St John Ambulance: p 112; Still Pictures: p 28 (bottom right) (Arbib); Summerhill School: p 35; Dr Richard Taylor: p 101; TimeBank: p 112

Every effort has been made to contact copyright holders. The publishers apologise to anyone whose rights have been inadvertently overlooked, and will be happy to rectify any errors or omissions.

The publisher has endeavoured to ensure that the URLs (website addresses) in this text are correct and active at the time of going to press. However, the publisher takes no responsibility for the websites, and cannot guarantee that a site will remain live or that the content is or will remain appropriate.

Contents

What is Citizenship?

Citizenship education is a very broad term which includes being able to find out information and developing your knowledge about society, how society works, and how individuals are affected by it. It is also about being able to make a difference yourself, developing as an active citizen and developing your own opinions about important issues in your community and around the world.

Using this book

Citizenship for You has been written to help you to gain the knowledge, understanding and skills necessary to pass the GCSE courses for Citizenship. There are a number of courses that lead to this particular qualification, and you should check which exam board you will be entered for, and familiarise yourself with their particular criteria, and the style of their exam papers. All courses are slightly different, and you need to be able to work towards the requirements of your particular exam board.

Active citizenship

All courses require you to have participated in an **active citizenship project**. This means that, more than any other course you may be studying for, Citizenship cannot be learnt completely from a textbook. As well as finding out about and discussing the issues covered, you have to actually **do** something. The active project could be based in the classroom, in the school, or in the wider community. You can do it on your own or with a group of people. Examples include:

- raising money for a charity
- helping to establish an environmental garden
- setting up links with other people or groups in the community
- contributing to a school/local newspaper
- writing a website for an organisation
- running a mini-enterprise scheme
- helping out at a reading club
- being a 'buddy' to help other students with problems
- setting up school-based campaigns to raise awareness about important issues
- participating in your school council

- arranging to meet local councillors to talk about community safety.

These are just a sample, and you can select from many other areas you are interested in. As you read through the book, think about the kinds of topic that interest you, and what sort of active projects you could carry out.

There is some help and guidance on how to plan, carry out and review your active experience in the first section of this book, but you will have to actually do the activity yourself, and this will require you to invest time and effort outside lesson time, and maybe outside the school.

Finding out

In addition to using this book you will need to use other sources of information. Newspapers, the internet, television and radio are all useful ways of keeping up with the issues you are studying. For example, if you are learning about Britain's relationship with the European Union, this book will provide you with some useful background information to help you understand stories that are currently in the news. Relationships like these will change over time, so your knowledge will also have to evolve and develop.

In addition to developing your knowledge through using the media, you will find it useful to discuss your ideas and opinions with other people in your class, and more broadly with people from outside the school. This means practising the skills of debate and discussion and testing your ideas against those of other people. When they ask you to justify your opinions and offer you alternative facts and figures, you should be able to see different points of view and become clearer about your own ideas. Learning from each other in this way is an important part of citizenship.

What you will learn

The book is divided into four sections. Each one covers different aspects of the syllabus.

Section 1 Citizenship Skills provides you with some ideas about the ways in which you may research citizenship issues. In some cases you will have to do your own research to find out about local issues, at other times you will have to employ skills that enable you to use information from other people. You will have to think about where information comes from, why it was produced and how useful it is to you. This section also provides some guidance for active citizenship and for debate and discussion. You should refer back to these pages as you work through the rest of the book, as the skills will be used throughout your course.

At the end of this section are some definitions of what levels you will be working at. These are only approximate and you should ask your teacher for grade descriptions for your syllabus for accurate information about what you are expected to do to achieve specific grades.

Section 2 Roles, Rights and Responsibilities should help you think about the nature of rights: What are they? What difference do they make? How do they relate to responsibilities? This section also looks at specific examples of rights in relation to education, equality, and the economy. These examples illustrate the ways in which rights are important in a range of situations.

By the end of this section you should have a clearer idea of what rights and responsibilities are and the difference they can make to our lives. You should also be able to understand some of the ways in which rights are often complicated and may come into conflict with one another.

Section 3 Government: Law Making, Shaping and Enforcing looks at the work of government and some of the changes that are happening in relation to how government is organised and how it carries out its work. Then we consider the ways in which laws are made and interpreted in the courts. Finally we consider some aspects of Britain's relations with the wider world.

By the end of this section you should have a clear idea of what government does, some of the ways in which the British government works with other governments and organisations around the world, and also an understanding of how the government makes and upholds the law.

Section 4 Active Citizens considers the ways in which people can influence their own lives and the lives of others. It starts with a look at voting – what it is, how it works and why it is important. It then moves on to consider how people can join together to achieve change through campaigning. This section ends with a case study on the environment which considers the ways in which change can be promoted, from our own kitchen sink to international governmental conferences.

By the end of this section you should have developed an understanding of the wide range of actions citizens can take to try to achieve their own objectives. You will also have had opportunities to think about how effective and acceptable different methods of active citizenship are likely to be.

Citizenship skills

This section of the book will help you think about the kinds of skills you need to develop in your Citizenship Studies. It is important that you do not just believe everything you are told, but this can go too far if you end up simply disbelieving everything instead. You will have to think about the evidence, and ask some questions about it, for example what does it tell you, what does it leave unsaid, what does it mean, who provided the information and why?

Obtaining and understanding evidence

Sources of evidence

Statistics

Some of the information you will use in your Citizenship Studies will come from tables and charts. You need to be able to make sense of them.

1 What is the table about?
2 What time-frame does the table cover?
3 What units of measurement are used?
4 Where does the information come from – what is the source?
5 When were the statistics in the table produced? (Could they be out of date?)
6 Does the table show any trends (patterns of change)? (For example, is reading becoming more popular?)

▽ Participation in home-based leisure activities: by gender, 1977–93/4 (percentages)

Activity	1977	1980	1986	1990/91	1993/94
Males					
Watching TV	97	97	98	99	99
Visiting/entertaining friends or relations	89	90	92	95	95
Listening to records/tapes	64	66	69	78	79
Reading books	52	52	52	56	59
Dressmaking/needlework/knitting	2	2	3	3	3
Females					
Watching TV	97	98	98	99	99
Visiting/entertaining friends or relations	93	93	95	97	96
Listening to radio	87	88	85	87	88
Reading books	57	61	64	68	71
Dressmaking/needlework/knitting	51	51	48	41	38

Source: *Social Trends* 1997, p.215

Understanding graphs and identifying trends

▽ Population living on less than $1 a day, excluding China

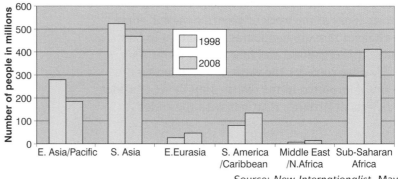

Source: *New Internationalist*, May 2001

Tasks

The most important details on any graphs are the title and labels. The graph above shows millions of people living in poverty.

1 What is expected to happen to the number of people living on less than $1 a day in South Asia?
2 What is expected to happen to the number of people living on less than $1 a day in Sub-Saharan Africa?
3 What trend does the chart show? Is poverty in most parts of the world expected to increase or decrease?

Different kinds of data and evidence

There are different types of information, and no golden rules about which are the most useful. It all depends on what questions you are asking and what you want the information for.

Conducting a street survey ▷

⚠ **Interesting, useful and often biased – we need to think when we read secondary sources**

Primary sources

Primary evidence is evidence produced by someone who was there at the time. It includes letters, diaries and eye-witness accounts. It is first-hand evidence. We often find primary evidence very interesting, but it cannot always be trusted. It is sometimes unreliable because:

● the emotions of the people involved might affect their judgement
● people can leave information out because they forget
● people can exaggerate for effect
● people sometimes have a biased (one-sided) view
● people are sometimes unaware of other facts and views at the time.

Primary data is information actually produced and collected by a researcher, e.g. questionnaires or interviews. Primary data is different from primary evidence because it is information actually produced by a researcher. Examples of primary data are:

● interviews
● questionnaires
● surveys
● participant observation.

These are explained in the next section.

Secondary sources

Secondary evidence is produced when someone reports information from other sources. Textbooks are a good example of secondary evidence. Secondary evidence can also be biased and unreliable because:

● authors may not have found sources of information that represent all views
● they may have reproduced the bias of primary sources
● they may have their own bias or opinion that they want to convince their reader about
● in attempting to summarise other people's opinions and arguments, it is easy to misrepresent them in some ways or oversimplify their point of view.

Secondary data, from the point of view of research, is information that already exists and has been produced or collected by other people. Examples of secondary data are:

● official statistics
● media reports.

Tasks ?

4 Write down as many points as you can think of in favour of using primary sources.

5 What kinds of primary evidence might you use for finding out about why young offenders commit crimes?

6 How would you gather primary data to find out about bullying in your school?

7 What secondary sources might you use to explore points of view about genetically modified (GM) foods?

Quantitative and qualitative data

Quantitative data is data presented in the form of numbers and is used a great deal in research about society. It is often produced through surveys and questionnaires. The graph below is an example. It shows the percentage of crimes committed that are actually reported to the police. You can see that only about a quarter of cases of vandalism were reported, but almost all cases of car theft were reported. Why do you think this might be?

▼ British crime statistics (BCS): proportion of offences reported to the police, 1997

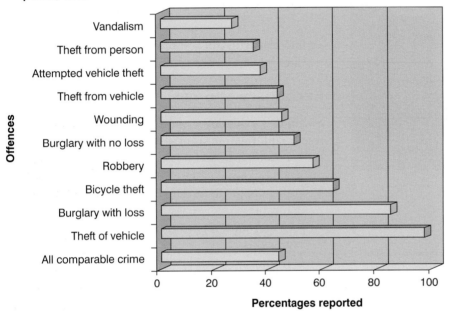

Offences (y-axis)

- Vandalism
- Theft from person
- Attempted vehicle theft
- Theft from vehicle
- Wounding
- Burglary with no loss
- Robbery
- Bicycle theft
- Burglary with loss
- Theft of vehicle
- All comparable crime

x-axis: 0 20 40 60 80 100
Percentages reported

▼ Some forms of information are striking but don't give us the 'whole picture'

Qualitative data is presented as words. It often tells us about how people feel about their experiences. Examples of qualitative data include in-depth interviews, diaries and letters. The extract below would count as qualitative data.

> ## School councils: The view of one student
>
> I came from a school which did not have a school council and I did not think it would make that much difference. But it does! We send tutor group representatives to the council... Sometimes we don't feel we get a fair hearing and we cannot discuss certain things such as uniform, but I would not want to go back to a school which did not have one, because on balance we are all treated equally and while it is not perfect it is better than many students have.

from a 1999 NSPCC report

Tasks

1 Where do you think the data in the graph comes from?
2 What questions would you find this data useful for?
3 What problems might there be with the data?
4 Could you use qualitative data to inform people about the reporting of crime?
5 What does the extract above tell you about the student's experiences and thoughts about school councils?
6 What is the advantage of using qualitative data for this topic?
7 What questions about school councils might be answered with quantitative data, and what questions would require qualitative data?

Doing your own research

Surveys – quantitative data

A **survey** is a series of questions that are given to the group of people from whom you want to gather data. The main kind of survey you will need to do for Citizenship Studies is a cross-sectional survey. If you are trying to find out about people's experiences or views of a particular issue, there are some steps you will need to take to make sure your evidence is valid.

First, you need to work out what your sample of people is going to be. If the group of people you are going to find out about (e.g. your own class) is fairly small, you will need to survey most of them to get an accurate picture. If it is larger (e.g. the year group) you will need a sample of over half the people. Below are some suggested sizes for random samples:

Size of population	Number to survey
10	10
30	28
200	132
1,000	278
1,000,000	384

These are the sample sizes recommended for professional research. Samples this size may be difficult for school students to obtain. However, it is important to be aware that if you are surveying a small 'population' your sample must be relatively big.

You also need to ensure that your sample represents the mixture of groups in the population, for example: gender, age, class and ethnicity.

Secondly, you need to decide on the kinds of questions you will ask. If you want to be able to show your findings in a statistical form, e.g. a graph, you will find it best to ask 'closed' questions. These are questions that offer a fixed set of given answers – often 'Yes', 'No' and 'Don't know'. They could also be questions that ask the respondents to tick from a list of identified boxes.

Tasks

In groups, complete the following tasks:

1 Draft a questionnaire for the class about their **experiences** of crime.
2 Draft a questionnaire for people on the high street about their **views** about crime.
3 List the advantages of surveys using 'closed' questions for finding out about issues.
4 List the disadvantages of this research method.

In-depth interviews – qualitative data

Some interviews can be tightly organised, with pre-planned questions. These are called **structured interviews**. They enable the researcher to find out more in-depth answers than questionnaires. It is also possible to go back and check answers if they are not clear.

An in-depth or unstructured interview is one in which the interviewer does not have a fixed set of questions and can follow up the interviewees' responses. This can provide more detail than other forms of research, but because every answer is likely to be very different it can make interviews more difficult to compare.

In-depth interviews are very useful for case studies. A **case study** is a piece of research where the researcher chooses one special group or situation and carries out a detailed study to find out about them.

Tasks

Working in groups:

5 List the advantages and disadvantages of in-depth interviews.
6 Try to think of three examples of issues where case studies might provide useful evidence.

Observation

Observation means watching and listening to the group you are studying. You record what you observe. Non-participant observation happens when the researcher does not join in.

▽ Non-participant observation sometimes affects people's behaviour. How might the behaviour of a class change when an inspector is in the room?

In participant observation, the researcher joins in with the group's activities, either openly or covertly (which means 'not letting on about the research'). The danger with participant observation is that if the researcher is too involved, the research can be biased. Covert observation can cause problems because it is considered dishonest to deceive people by not letting them know about the research.

An example of participant observation is studies of football hooliganism where the researchers pretend to be football fans.

▽ Participant covert observation can have some problems

Discussion 💬

Discuss in your group:

- Why would participant observation be useful for finding out about gangs?
- How might this be better than covert non-participant observation?
- What problems might the researchers face with participant observation?

Other primary data – audio-visual evidence

You may want to collect audio-visual evidence for your research. This can include:

- photographs
- tape recordings
- videos.

Skills for working with evidence

As you gain experience in working with evidence, you will be able to show higher levels of thinking in your work. You will be able to show that you can do some of the things at the end of this list:

1 You can answer simple questions about specific facts.
2 You can explain what some of the information means.
3 You can say how the information relates to and compares or contrasts with other information.
4 You can say what information might be missing.
5 You can tell the opinion of the person who produced the information.
6 You can explain why this person might hold this view.
7 You can explain why particular sources are reliable or unreliable.
8 You can organise the information to provide your own account.
9 You can decide which sources are useful for your investigation and explain why.
10 You can draw your own conclusions and make your own judgements about the issues and the sources.

Set yourself targets for your own skill development from this list as you work with evidence.

Now try to apply some of these skills to the two sources on this page. Both were produced during a period of argument about the state of the National Health Service. This was provoked by the treatment of a 94-year-old patient whose relatives blamed the hospital for neglect.

Source A

> ### People are rightly angry that Rose Addis, 94, was left in casualty for 3 days
>
> There is a REAL issue here. A REAL scandal.
>
> It is that the apparatus of the state has united behind the HOSPITAL not the PATIENT.
>
> Rose has been made to look a racist, her family have been smeared as uncaring.
>
> After 4 days on the attack – and after the Health Secretary described Rose's complaints as 'fiction' – the Government is made to look foolish as the hospital issues a grudging apology.
>
> And it is revealed that an independent report has criticised standards, waiting times and staffing levels at the Whittington. It appears this god-forsaken hospital doesn't even change the SHEETS on beds between patients.

from *The Sun*, 26 January 2002

Source B

> " … The patient was kept in a medical assessment unit. The hospital states that that is a perfectly proper way of looking after her. … in-patient waiting lists have fallen by more than 100,000 since this government came to office. Under the previous, Conservative government, the numbers of nurses and doctors in training and the number of beds were cut. In the past year, the government has been increasing the number of beds and we have increased the number of nurses and doctors in training. "

from a speech by Prime Minister Tony Blair on 24 January 2002

Tasks

1 Take note of where each source comes from. We call this **provenance**. The provenance of a source often tells us whether or not it is reliable, and can indicate how it might be biased.
2 List all the facts you can find from both sources.
3 Now note any opinions you can find.
4 Can you find any examples of bias (a one-sided view)?
5 Now look at who wrote or said these things. What does the author want us to believe? How is this shown in their language?
6 Comment on the reliability of the sources – give reasons why you might, or might not, trust each source.
7 What other information would you need to make a judgement about whether the criticisms of the National Health Service are fair?
8 These sources may be unreliable, but can you explain why they are useful?

Taking action – making a difference

Active citizenship cycle

Citizenship is about taking action to make a difference. This could involve setting up a recycling system in your school, making a presentation about crime in your community, or joining a campaign to target a global issue. It's your chance to have a say and make a difference in the world around you. Whatever you decide to do, here are six easy steps to help you.

Step 1: What bothers you?

What bothers you in your school, in your local area or the world? What would you like to change? Or is there something successful that you would like to build on? Make a list of the things you would really like to change or improve.

Appreciative inquiry

Instead of looking at problems, why not focus on what is good about your area? Find out what works or what people like, and do more of it.

Video and photography

Take a camera or a video camera and explore your school or local area. Video or take photos of:
● the things or areas you like or dislike
● the things or areas that could be improved.

Probable/possible futures

On a large piece of paper, draw two timelines, which cover the next five years. One line should represent what is *likely to happen* in the next five years (the probable future), the other represents what *you would like to happen* (the possible future). If your answers are different, think about what you could change to help make the 'possible future' happen.

Step 2: Choosing an issue

Now look through your list of issues and for each one, ask yourself: Is it relevant? Is it realistic?

Is this issue relevant to other people? If you choose an issue that other people are concerned about, your project will have more relevance and support.

Is there a realistic chance that you can change this issue? It may help to investigate what is going on in your school or local area at the moment. For example, if your school has money to spend on the school grounds, it would be a good time to do a project on improving the school grounds.

Is it realistic to change this issue in the time you have been given? Remember, things often take a long time to change.

Start small, but think big!

Step 3: Investigating the issue

Once you have chosen a relevant and realistic issue that you would like to change, you will need to find out more about it and collect evidence to support your ideas for change.

You will be more successful in changing your issue if you can show that it is a major problem and that many other people support your ideas. Use the research techniques on pages 6–11 to investigate your issue. Primary research can include organising a survey using questionnaires, video or photos, or a petition.

Use secondary research as additional evidence to support your argument.

Step 4: Action planning

Fill in an 'Influence Tree' like the example below, to start planning for change.

- **Example of an 'Influence Tree'**

- **What is the change we want?**
  We want the top five supermarkets to change their policy on bananas and to sell only fair trade bananas.

- **Who has the power to make the change?**

- **Who can influence them?**

- **What can *we* do?**

- What do we want to change? Project aim: …
- Who has the power to make this change?
- Who can influence them and help us?

Supermarket Board of Directors

Public relations department | Shareholders | Branch managers

National media | Customers | Local media | Staff

Put on a play or street theatre | Inform our parents | Take coupons into the store | Save till-receipts and write a letter | Talk and inform

Step 5: Taking action

Now you are ready to think about how you are going to achieve your project goal. There are many ways to take action for change. For example, if your issue is the lack of recycling facilities in your area, you can:
- set up a scheme to recycle paper in school
- raise awareness of the importance of recycling by producing posters
- make a presentation to the local council to demand more recycling centres.

Brainstorm as many ideas as you can, but remember: they must be realistic and relevant.

If you are working in a group, it will help to use an action planning grid like the one below to plan your project.

Now go out and do it!

Priorities for investigation/action	What kind of evidence will be shown?	Who will do it?	When will it be done?

Step 6: Reflect and review

When you have finished your project, it is important to think through what you did, and to discuss the following questions with your group. This will help you to be even more successful next time!

- Did we achieve our goal? How do we know?
- What would we do differently next time?
- What have we learnt about changing things?
- How well did we work together as a group?
- What new skills have we learnt?

Critical thinking

Critical thinking and the media

We are constantly bombarded with information, news and views – from the TV, radio, newspapers, films and the internet. The amount of information available to us is growing faster than ever before because of modern communications, and especially the internet. What we see and hear on the news depends on the views of those who produce it. If we are going to make sense of all this information, we need to be able to think critically about it.

Critical thinking involves asking good questions and spotting bad answers. If you are thinking critically about the information you receive, you will ask yourself:

1 Who has produced this information?
2 Are the 'facts' accurate? What parts of this information are facts? What are opinions?
3 Why is this view or opinion being expressed?
4 What information am I *not* being given?
5 How does this information relate to what I have heard elsewhere?

Task

Find an example of a news story: it could be about politics or music or film stars – anything you know something about. Ask yourself the questions listed on this page. Write down the answers and compare your answers with those of others in the class.

Now apply these questions to the media:

1 Who has produced this information? Who owns the company that is producing this news?

Only six companies control the majority of the world's media – including newspapers, magazines, TV, films, music, books and the internet.

2 Are the facts accurate? What parts of this information are facts? Which are opinions?

Check them out. Too often, facts are manipulated or just plain wrong.

3 Why is this view or opinion being expressed?

The media is not neutral. All newspapers, for example, reflect certain political positions and it is important to know this in order to spot bias.

4 What information am I not being given?

A lot of news is simply not covered. Often international news is not considered very important. In fact, in Europe and America international news coverage has dropped on average by 50% in the last ten years.

5 How does this information relate to what I have heard elsewhere?

Because the media is not neutral, it is important to make sure you get your information from more than one source.

Asylum-seekers and the media

Asylum-seekers have become a major issue in the news. Some newspapers have taken a firm stand against them. They use strong language, suggesting for example that Britain is being 'flooded' by 'bogus' asylum-seekers and 'scroungers'. It is easy to get the impression that we are under threat, but take a critical look at the facts and another story emerges.

The facts

The following facts have been selected by the Refugee Council to help you think about the kinds of opinions that commonly appear in newspapers. (You can see more examples at: **www.refugeecouncil.org.uk**.) This selection of facts shows you how easy it is to present a different view of an issue, depending on your selection of facts.

- How do each of the facts below relate to the extracts from newspapers on the left (below)?
- How easy is it to spot that the following statements come from an organisation that supports refugees and asylum-seekers' rights?

We resent the scroungers, beggars and crooks who are prepared to cross every country in Europe to reach our generous benefits system

from *The Sun*, 7 March 2001

Many will undoubtedly have been hoping to end up in Britain, the number one asylum destination for asylum-seekers

from *The Daily Telegraph*, 19 February 2001

Asylum cheats are a threat to our future

from *Mail on Sunday*, 4 March 2001

1 Asylum-seekers are not allowed to work in the first six months of their asylum application. After that they are given the right to work — not the jobs themselves. In fact, many asylum-seekers have skills and experience which could make a significant contribution to our economy and culture.

2 Asylum-seekers receive only 70% of basic income support. So asylum-seekers are forced to live 30% below the poverty line.

3 The world's poorest countries receive the most asylum-seekers. For example, Iran and Pakistan each host over 2 million refugees from Afghanistan. Britain had just 76,000 new arrivals in 1999.

4 Britain has signed the UN Convention on Refugees, which means that anyone has the legal right to come to this country and claim asylum.

The world through their eyes

Empathetic thinking

Empathy, or **empathetic thinking**, is about seeing the world through the eyes of someone else. Empathy is more than sympathy. It means trying to see things from the standpoint of someone else, imagining that you share their life and circumstances, and see the world as they do. This is an important citizenship skill, because it is much easier to solve problems when we understand other people's points of view.

One way to develop our empathetic thinking is to use role play. Role play can be used any time you want to try and see the world through someone else's eyes. When you use role play you should:

1 make sure the roles you play represent as many sides of the issue as possible
2 make sure the information you have about the roles is accurate
3 take a few minutes to get into role and really empathise with the individual
4 make it clear when you are in role and when you have come out of role.

Different people respond differently to different situations. So we cannot just ask ourselves the simple question: How would I feel if this happened to me? It is also important to ask questions about other people's actual lives – the culture they live in, their personal history and the way they feel. For example, if you were a bride at a traditional English wedding and people started pinning money all over your dress you might be offended, whereas if you were at a traditional Greek wedding you would expect it.

The case studies on the opposite page represent different views and experiences of people relating to the issue of asylum-seekers and refugees.

Discussion

• In your group, discuss how you think we should treat people who come to the UK to seek asylum.

• Divide the roles up randomly within your group – each person should have one role. Now continue your discussion from the point of view of the role you are playing. Use the quotes to get you thinking and then, using empathy, develop the roles, adding your own details about family background, current experiences and hopes for the future.

• Change roles in your group and continue the discussion from the point of view you are now playing.

• When you have stopped your role play, think again about how we should treat people who come to the UK to seek asylum. Have you changed your views at all? If so, what made you change them? If not, why not?

Thinking about asylum as a citizenship issue

Refugees and asylum-seekers are an important area of citizenship study. They reflect our role in the world; the government is constantly discussing what to do for the best; and yet every asylum-seeker has their own experiences and reasons for leaving their country that makes them unique. Everyone seems to have an opinion on the subject.

Look back over the previous pages and think about what has helped to influence your opinion.

Test case

Many refugees have been forced from their homes by war. They may only have a few minutes to grab their belongings and leave. They have no idea when or if they will ever return.

Imagine that your community was under attack and you were forced to flee. Make a list of the five most important things you would take with you. Remember, you have to carry them yourself. Write them down in a list.

Now imagine you have been robbed on your way through a dangerous region. The second and third items on your list have been stolen. How would you feel?

Do you think your list would have been different if you came from another country, or from a poor farming family? How might it differ?

Omar, an Iraqi Kurd:
asylum-seeker

I've been living here in Dover now for nearly ten months. It's not easy because it is a small town and refugees can be easily recognised. The only people I've met who are friendly belong to the council, or social services or organisations... You are not accepted and you are not welcomed by people.

We had this idea of Britain being a nice place. People think it's nice and easy, and that you've got help there. But the minute they come in they realise how difficult it is. I used to stand in the playground and not talk to anybody. It was difficult not knowing the language and not knowing anybody. I just felt: What do you do? How do you fit in? How do you move forward? Nobody understands you.

Hannah, 19:
refugee

**Joyce Valender, 69 and
Sheila Broughton, 60:**
English pensioners

They ought to send them all home. The government gave us pensioners a 73p a week rise in April but they can always find money for these people. They ought to be sent straight back. They're not asylum-seekers, they just want an easy life.

The Sun newspaper: editorial

Scroungers, illegal immigrants and criminals are sucking this country dry. The cost of this multi-billion pound racket is staggering. And it is hard-working taxpayers who are footing the bill... Our land is being swamped by a flood of fiddlers stretching our resources and patience to breaking point. We need deportations on a huge scale... Britain has had enough.

Whatever else these individuals are, they are not 'economic migrants' involved in some frivolous action to gain the dubious joys of a dodgy bed and breakfast hotel in one of Britain's inner cities and a long wait on vouchers.

Nick Hardwick:
Chief Executive, Refugee Council

Argument and discussion

You may have been told once too often to 'Stop arguing!' In citizenship, argument is actively encouraged, as long as you also listen to what other people are saying and show respect towards them. Argument does not mean shouting or simply repeating your own view; it means engaging with the views of others, and responding to them.

Whether you are discussing which is the best football team in Britain, or watching politicians on the news arguing about national issues in the Houses of Parliament, you will know that discussion is a vital part of our lives. Discussion and argument are also essential for active citizenship. If you are not able express your views effectively, how will you persuade anyone that what you have to say is important? And if you are unable to convince others of the importance of your opinion, how will you get them to support you or help you to change anything?

Meaningful discussion is a skill everyone needs to learn. The ideas below will help you build these skills. Before you start an important discussion, you will need to take plenty of time to prepare.

- You will need a strong argument supported by relevant facts.

- You will need to know the views of the people you will be arguing against so that you can respond effectively.

- You will need to be able to listen carefully to what others are saying and be prepared to accept that someone may have a better argument than you.

- You will need to be open-minded and ready to change your own opinion.

Debate tactics

There are many tactics you can use when debating. Obviously the most important one is to have evidence to support your point of view. In Citizenship courses this is a basic skill that you will have to practise and which you must use in your own writing as well. But when you are having a debate and several different opinions are being expressed, there are other techniques you can use.

Fault the logic
Show that the conclusion does not follow from the evidence presented.

Refer to the law
Use national or international laws to support your case.

Question the evidence
Argue that the evidence is wrong, biased, or has ignored important facts.

Appeal to authority
Refer to someone who is recognised as an expert who supports your position.

DEBATE

Use personal examples
Use examples of individuals to illustrate your point.

Admit the point
Admit that the person has a good point and then go on to make a new or different point.

Put the issue in context
Use facts or figures to put the issue in context.

Discussion

1 Read the discussion statement below and try to match responses with the discussion tactics on page 18.
2 Working in pairs or small groups, choose a discussion statement about a topic on which you all have an opinion, and try to come up with a response using one of the discussion tactics.

3 Using the ideas on the next page, have a classroom debate in two teams **for** and **against** a discussion statement.

DISCUSSION STATEMENT

'Cannabis should be legalised because so many people are now smoking it that it is impossible to maintain the law, and because it is harmless.'

Just because a group of people break the law does not make it acceptable. Street crime is increasing but no-one would suggest that the solution is to stop it being a crime because it is so common.

But many more people do not use it, and besides there is some evidence that it may have long-term effects on memory.

But look at the example of that driver who crashed his car and hurt those children on the school crossing last month. He had been smoking cannabis and it shows the kind of thing that would happen if cannabis was allowed out in the open.

Over 90% of young male offenders and 75% of females use alcohol or drugs. Making cannabis legal will just increase young people's access to this side of life and therefore feed into the problem of youth crime more generally.

It may well be safe and widespread. But the real point is that cannabis is just the first step on the road to more serious drug abuse. If we relax the law here (even though there may seem to be good arguments for it) we will simply create more problems for the future.

Numerous government ministers and committees of experts have looked at this problem. They all agree that the evidence is inconclusive. Who are we to presume we know more than them?

There are many rights that we have and which should be protected by the government. Taking drugs is not one of our rights and the government is therefore justified in protecting us from the harm drugs may do.

For and against

Debate

Discussion and argument are things we all do every day. When our discussions become more formal and specific we may call them a **debate**. A debate is a formal discussion about a specific issue. Debates usually centre on a **motion** – a discussion statement that gives a certain view about an issue. Two teams then debate the issue: one team is **for** the issue and the other **against** it. At the end of the debate, the audience will often vote for or against the issue. Whether the debate involves politicians in the Houses of Parliament, or you in your classroom, there are some simple steps to follow. The diagram below shows you the different parts you can play in a debate.

Chairperson
- Should be fair and firm enough to keep order
- Must explain the motion
- Should introduce the speakers in order
- Should invite people from the audience to have their say or ask questions
- Must take a vote on the motion, asking the audience if they are for or against the motion

Speaker 1
- Should speak FOR the motion for 3 minutes
- Should be able to answer questions from the audience
- Should be able to summarise the whole argument FOR the motion at the end of the debate

Speaker 3
- Should speak FOR the motion for 2 minutes
- Should be able to answer questions from the audience

Speaker 4
- Should speak AGAINST the motion for 2 minutes
- Should be able to answer questions from the audience

Speaker 2
- Should speak AGAINST the motion for 3 minutes
- Should be able to answer questions from the audience
- Should be able to summarise the whole argument AGAINST the motion at the end of the debate

Audience
- Listen to the speeches
- Ask questions of the speakers at the end of the speeches
- Make their own short comments or statements about the motion at the end

Discussion

Work together as a class.

1 Decide on a motion to debate. For example:
- 'Britain should limit the number of asylum-seekers it accepts each year.'
- 'The Royal Family should be abolished.'
- 'Cannabis should be made fully legal.'

2 Decide who will take on each role for the debate.

3 Take time to read through the information in the previous pages about critical thinking, empathy and discussion tactics. This will help you prepare your speeches.

4 Hold the class debate and vote on the motion at the end.

Presentation tips

If you have the best speech in the world, but cannot present your views clearly, you will fail to convince the audience of your argument. Think about these tips to help you present your views in the most powerful way.

Volume – make sure everyone can hear you!

Eye contact – try not to bury your head in your notes. Look at the audience as much as possible.

Speed – speak slowly and clearly.

Visual aids – use visual aids such as overhead projectors, PowerPoint or video to support your argument. But test it out beforehand.

Remember the Golden Rule:
Start by saying what you are going to say. Then say it. Finish by saying what you've said.

Debate tips

Before you start writing, think about the motion you are discussing. What is the 'sense' of the motion – what is it about and what ideas is it supporting? Often there are several parts to a motion, and you may wish to think about each part separately.

For example:

> MOTION:
>
> 'The EU should open its borders.'
>
> SENSE:
>
> 1 EU countries have a duty to accept those who are fleeing political persecution, recognising the rights of the individuals who seek refuge.
>
> 2 The EU countries rarely do more than their basic requirement.
>
> 3 There are advantages to allowing more immigrants to enter the EU just because they want to work. In this way they benefit from having better jobs, and the EU countries benefit from having hard workers.

Discussion

Review

Once you have held a formal debate, review your strengths and think about your weaknesses. Ask others in the class to give you some feedback.
You could think about the following skills:

Planning	Talking	Arguing	Responding	Presenting

Target setting and action planning

When you come to the end of a term or a module, it is important to make judgements about how you are doing in the course. You can also support your classmates in assessing their performance. There are three main objectives you are being judged against. These are:

1 Knowledge and understanding of citizenship issues and how these affect our lives.
2 Investigating issues, working with evidence, debating and discussing.
3 Planning and evaluating your skills of participation – working with others to change things.

The GCSE grades for all the exam boards that offer Citizenship Studies are based on your performance in these areas. These pages will help you think about what grade you are working at, and what you need to do for a higher grade.

Example 1: Debating and discussing

The extracts below describe what a candidate has to do for each grade in discussion and debate.

Grade F
Candidates have taken part in discussions and can express opinions with reasons.

Grade A
Candidates recognise how complicated many issues are. They weigh up opinions and make judgements using a wide range of evidence and well-developed arguments.

It should be obvious which student is going to get the higher grade. Look at each contribution and answer the questions in the Tasks box.

Tasks

1 Explain why Imelda's work is better than Billy's.
2 What advice would you give to Billy to improve his grade?
3 Imelda's work is good, but do you think it does all the things required for a grade A?
4 What advice could you give Imelda to improve her work and guarantee a grade A?

> I think cannabis should be legalised because it doesn't seem to be any more dangerous than alcohol, and that is legal.

Billy

> You should believe in the legalisation of cannabis if you respect the law. Policing a drug that causes so little harm is a drain on police resources, it clogs up the courts as time is wasted on dealing with petty offenders, and very few serious sentences are passed out anyway. It also contributes to a growing disrespect for the law. If people see one law being broken day after day, why should they take other laws seriously? The law is not fixed for ever, it changes and develops with society. Things that were illegal before, such as women attending university, are legal today, and things that were legal, such as corporal punishment in school, are illegal today. When the law reflects how people live their lives, it works better.

Imelda

Target setting

Both Billy and Imelda could set personal targets to improve their answer. To be useful, a target has to do more than say 'Get better at debating'. It has to be **SMART**:

Specific

Measurable

Achievable

Realistic

Time-related.

Write an example of a specific target for each of the candidates. Remember, it is unlikely that anyone will leap from a grade F to an A, so targets should plan for step-by-step progress.

Example 2: Reflecting on active citizenship

The following extracts from the grade descriptions describe performance in relation to your active citizenship project.

Grade F

Candidates provide evidence that they have taken part with others in school and/or community activities, and reflected on their participation.

Grade C

Candidates evaluate their participation in school and/or community activities, providing evidence of their ability to work with others.

Grade A

Candidates critically evaluate their participation in school and/or community activities, providing evidence of their ability to work with, and help, others.

Billy, Imelda and their friend Jasmine have all participated in the same project.

The group heard that their head teacher was going to redevelop the school canteen. As far as they knew, there were no plans to discuss what students wanted and so the group went to see the head. They asked if they could carry out a survey to find out what other students wanted from the canteen redevelopment, and she agreed. She invited them to present their findings to the governors' meeting, where the plans and budget would be approved. This would give the governors the chance to ask any questions of Billy, Imelda and Jasmine.

Tasks

Once they had written up their coursework the students got the following grades:

Billy (F)   Jasmine (C)   Imelda (A).

1 Divide into groups of three, with each member of the group taking one character. Write a summary of the coursework for each character, which you think would match the grade that they received.
2 Compare your work with that of others in your group, and discuss what each person did well in their report and what they could improve on.
3 Working as a group, write up a list of rules to follow for writing up good coursework.
4 Share your list with the others in the class, and try to come up with the best advice you can to help everyone in the class get the best grade possible.

What are roles?

Human beings generally live together in social groups. Only in exceptional cases – as when children have been brought up by animals, or adults choose to live as hermits – are there no social links between people.

Within these social groups, people act in particular ways. They take on roles within the group. Roles usually have responsibilities attached to them.

Roles in families

Within a family, roles can be determined by who you are related to (mother and daughter, for example), or by what your responsibilities are (wage earner or home maker, for example). When the roles are clearly understood and accepted by everybody, then people generally find it easier to live together in harmony. If roles are not agreed, there may be conflict. For example, if an older child tries to take on a disciplinary role in relation to the younger children in the family, this may cause confusion.

These pictures show different family groupings around the world. What are the likely roles of different members of the families shown here?

Friends' roles

In a similar way, there can be different sets of roles between groups of friends. You may depend on different friends for different things, and friends also have responsibilities towards each other – like trust, and support.

Roles in the community

Larger social groups work in the same way. In a village, town or nation, members of communities interact and depend on each other – although this may not be obvious to everyone involved. Social roles can be determined by culture. For example, community members in a new township in a Latin American city often take on roles as organisers and developers – such roles are less common in residential areas of European cities. Where there is a tradition of community self-help, people work easily together to try and achieve commonly agreed aims. Such collaboration is a social role, showing members' sense of responsibility towards each other.

School roles

In school we have certain roles to play too. The teachers' role brings with it the responsibility of helping students to develop, and keeping them safe. Students may have a variety of roles in school but generally they have the responsibility to be well behaved and not disrupt the learning of others. Parents have responsibilities for making sure that their children receive an education, either in school or through alternative provision.

Learning roles

Children learn their roles in the family and community from the earliest age. They are **socialised** into the ways they relate to members of their family and to other people. This means that they learn from what they see going on around them. In many societies, this is aided by adults who are not their natural parents: by aunts, uncles and grandparents. Children may be informally fostered for extended periods of time and grow up with another member of that **extended family**.

Many societies distinguish clearly between roles for boys and for girls. Among the Maasai in East Africa, boys learn from older males skills in managing herds of cattle, while girls learn from older females skills in home building and craft-working. Young people then go through initiation ceremonies to mark their taking on of adult roles. In most European societies today, such changes in roles and responsibilities are less clearly marked out by the group's members. The whole group may not even be involved in the ceremonies, for example on the occasion of an 18th birthday party, which often marks entry into adult roles in British society.

'What roles do I have?' ▷

Tasks

1 What responsibilities do you have (if any) to:
   a other members of your family?
   b your friends?
   c people in school?
2 How have your roles in your family, at school or amongst your friends changed over the years? Explain how your own roles have changed, and how this has affected you.
3 What new responsibilities do you think you will have in the future?

Discussion

Use the photographs opposite to set up a role-play debate between different types of family. This could be organised as a meeting of a 'World Summit on Families'.
* Each family should present itself to the whole meeting, explaining who does what in the family.
* Families should then put questions to individual members of other families: What roles do they have? Do they enjoy them?

Think about how family roles are influenced by factors like **environment** and **tradition**.

YOUTH CLUB

Everyone has rights

When people in families and communities have expectations about how they should be treated by others, we call these expectations **rights**. Because I belong to a group I feel I have the **right** to be respected, to be listened to, to be treated fairly, and so on – in other words, to be accepted as an equal member of the group, who contributes to it and expects to take from it.

In the language of rights this is called 'respecting the rights of others'. It is seen as the natural consequence of having your own rights respected. If I have the right to speak and state my opinions, then I should be able to accept that others have the same right. When everyone agrees that all in the group have these rights, then the social group works. This brings us back to the idea of responsibility: having the **right** to speak implies at the same time having the **responsibility** of listening to others.

Nation states are large communities which often set out the rights that members can expect to have respected. This is like creating a set of rules so that everyone knows what kind of social behaviour is expected of them in order for the society to work well. Examples of these are constitutional documents like **Bills of Rights** which give citizens the rights to freedom of expression, choice of government, and so on. Citizens therefore have the power to remove governments that are seen to abuse their agreed rights.

RIGHTS

We need to demand....

control over our natural resources.

good medical care within easy reach and community control over how, what and when health services are offered

the right to work at home to ensure a whole, healthy society

information about health threats like AIDS and other sexually transmitted diseases; alcoholism and smoking

RESPONSIBILITIES

We must take responsibility for:

spending wages wisely;

building up strong VIDCOs and District Councils that are answerable to the people

using and conserving our natural resources for the benefit of local people now and for future generations.

our own health; preventing disease and death by immunizing children, using home-based remedies like diarrhoea mixture, taking children to the clinic (or the doctor) as soon as they get sick

▲ One community's view of its rights and responsibilities

Some countries – the United Kingdom was a well-known example until very recently – have chosen not to state all rights agreed for citizens. British law, with its many cases and precedents, lays down the limits of what rights citizens have and what may happen if they infringe the rights of others. Over the years the UK has signed up to many international agreements – one example is the *United Nations Convention on the Rights of the Child* – without absorbing them into British law.

However, the *European Convention on Human Rights* has recently been made into UK law as the Human Rights Act 1998. So citizens of the UK now have an agreed set of rights to refer to in any disagreements between individual citizens and the state. One example of conflict over rights is whether parents hitting their children infringes the children's right to 'liberty and security'. Another example would be the interception of e-mail messages, which could be seen as breaking the 'right to respect for private life'.

Universal rights?

The picture opposite is from Zimbabwe in southern Africa. It shows one community's view of the rights and responsibilities of its members. (VIDCOs are village development committees.)

Policing rights

The cartoon above suggests that it is not always easy to ensure that people have their rights. What else could the family in the picture do?

Tasks

1 Brainstorm all the things that come into your mind when you think of 'rights'. Share your responses to the word 'rights' with a partner in the class. Do you have the same ideas? Can you agree on a definition of what a 'right' is?
2 a Write five sentences beginning: 'If I have a right to …, then I have a responsibility to …'.
  b Do you agree that rights should be matched with responsibilities?
  c Can you think of an example when you have claimed a right but you did not take on the responsibility that goes with it?

Discussion

What would it be like to live in a country where no-one felt they had any rights or responsibilities?

Extension

Not everyone in the world has all their rights upheld and respected by their government.
• Find an example of rights abuse anywhere in the world, and present your case to the rest of the class.
• Hold a classroom discussion on what action could be taken to try to overcome the problems that have been presented. Think about the role of charities, governments and the United Nations.
• You may find it useful to visit **www.amnesty.org.uk** to identify some case studies.

Two views of rights

A brief history of human rights

We can look at the way rights have developed over time.

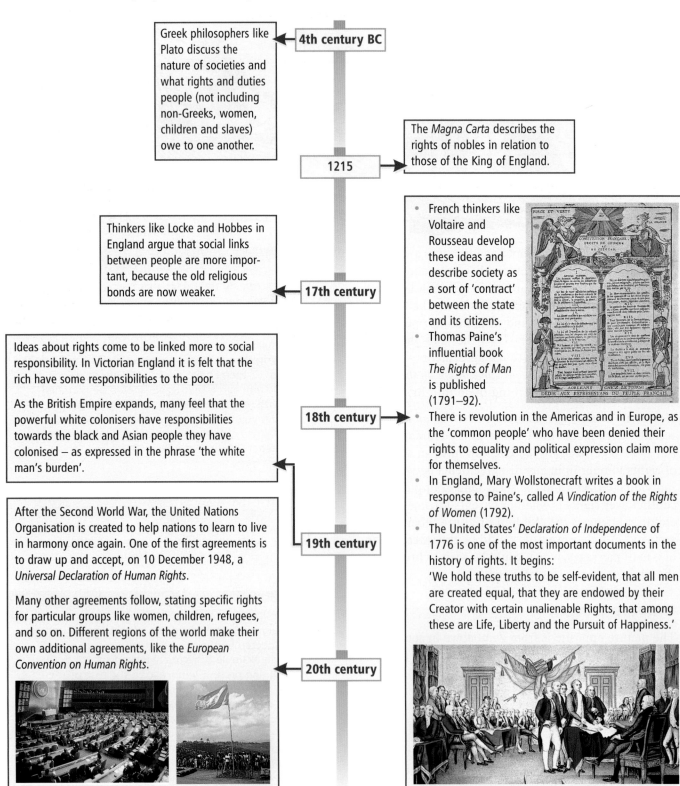

Greek philosophers like Plato discuss the nature of societies and what rights and duties people (not including non-Greeks, women, children and slaves) owe to one another.

4th century BC

1215

The *Magna Carta* describes the rights of nobles in relation to those of the King of England.

Thinkers like Locke and Hobbes in England argue that social links between people are more important, because the old religious bonds are now weaker.

17th century

• French thinkers like Voltaire and Rousseau develop these ideas and describe society as a sort of 'contract' between the state and its citizens.

• Thomas Paine's influential book *The Rights of Man* is published (1791–92).

Ideas about rights come to be linked more to social responsibility. In Victorian England it is felt that the rich have some responsibilities to the poor.

As the British Empire expands, many feel that the powerful white colonisers have responsibilities towards the black and Asian people they have colonised – as expressed in the phrase 'the white man's burden'.

18th century

• There is revolution in the Americas and in Europe, as the 'common people' who have been denied their rights to equality and political expression claim more for themselves.

• In England, Mary Wollstonecraft writes a book in response to Paine's, called *A Vindication of the Rights of Women* (1792).

• The United States' *Declaration of Independence* of 1776 is one of the most important documents in the history of rights. It begins:

'We hold these truths to be self-evident, that all men are created equal, that they are endowed by their Creator with certain unalienable Rights, that among these are Life, Liberty and the Pursuit of Happiness.'

After the Second World War, the United Nations Organisation is created to help nations to learn to live in harmony once again. One of the first agreements is to draw up and accept, on 10 December 1948, a *Universal Declaration of Human Rights*.

Many other agreements follow, stating specific rights for particular groups like women, children, refugees, and so on. Different regions of the world make their own additional agreements, like the *European Convention on Human Rights*.

19th century

20th century

Different types of rights

Whilst some people tend to focus on the development of rights over time, it is also possible to think about rights as different types:

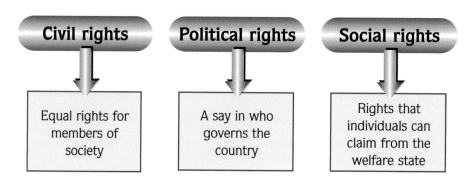

Civil rights	Political rights	Social rights
Equal rights for members of society	A say in who governs the country	Rights that individuals can claim from the welfare state

Where do the following examples of rights fit into this 'classification'?

Equality before the courts

Right to vote

Unemployment benefit

Right to meet with others and join organisations

Equal rights to own land

Free education

National Health Service

Right to criticise government

Right to stand as a candidate in elections

Can you think of any other rights to add under these headings?

Tasks

1 Read again the famous quotation from the US *Declaration of Independence* on page 28. Write down any words or phrases that you find difficult to understand, or which you think are old-fashioned uses of English. Then try to re-word this claim of rights in your own words, as a modern-day English version. For example, how would you now choose to re-word 'all men...'?

2 Make notes or an illustrated diagram about key events in the history of rights. Try to add what you think might be key events in the near future (for example, think about particular groups that still do not have all their rights respected).

3 Make a list of all the rights people should have (you may include as many as you wish). Refer to key documents like the Universal Declaration of Human Rights for guidance (you can find this Declaration at: www.un.org/Overview/rights.html). Go through your list and decide which rights are civil, political and social.

Extension

What have you learnt about the history of rights during your school years? Make a presentation for your Citizenship teacher about what you think should be taught on this subject, and why you think it is valuable for all young people to learn about rights.

What about rights for young people?

Are rights important? Could societies function and people get on together without defining their rights? Most people would say that a set of agreed principles makes things easier. Where rights are defined and accepted, it is easier to challenge any abuse and violation of basic human values.

There are still people struggling for their full rights in the UK: such as refugees and asylum-seekers, people with disabilities, gays and lesbians – and children. Although the UK has been a signatory of the UN *Convention on the Rights of the Child* for over ten years, rights of children and young people are still not fully respected by all adults – as these examples from a recent survey of young people's opinions suggest.

We have the right to go into public places: sometimes they won't let you go into swimming pools and things because you haven't got an adult with you.

The law on people abusing children should be a lot stronger. They do it because they think they can get away with it. We're not as strong as adults. They think they can pick on us.

Racism should be kicked out. I'd be walking down the street and people would just shout, 'Oi Paki!' – I've heard that so many times.

Young people shouldn't have to live on the streets because they can't get money. The Government should help.

I should like to know why we don't know about what rights we have.

If you're in a wheelchair, they laugh at you. They say, he's stupid.

It's not fair just having 18-year-olds being able to vote. If you pay tax and National Insurance, you should have a vote, a say in what's happening, where your money's going.

▼ Images of rights

Tasks

1 Take each of the young people's opinions stated on page 30 in turn, and say how much you agree or disagree with them.
2 Are there other ways in which young people's access to rights in the UK could be improved?
3 Look at the illustrations on this page. Which right do you think each one is illustrating?
4 Write a short statement on ways in which you think young people's rights could be better protected by:
   a young people
   b adults.

Extension

You feel that one of your rights is not being properly respected. What do you do? Choose *one* of the pictures on this page and develop a scenario. This could be done as a drama in a small group. Show your drama to the whole class. Ideally do it again, only this time people can stop the action and suggest other developments. After the dramas, discuss how real the situations and outcomes you created are, and how you can be champions for your own rights and for the rights of others.

Children's rights in the family

◁▽ **What different roles are people likely to have in these different types of family?**

What is a family?

All families are different. Can you define who *your* family is? For some young people, 'family' may mean just themselves and one parent. For others, it may mean a large group of brothers and sisters, parents and step-parents, aunts, uncles, cousins and grandparents living together, in the same neighbourhood, or scattered around the country or even the world. Others may have no blood relatives. Does that mean they have no family?

Young people have a wide range of different roles, rights and responsibilities within the family, depending on who they live with, the number of people in their family, their ages, religious beliefs and culture. So is it possible to say that some rights and responsibilities within a family group are universal to all young people?

Are these rights that all young people should have?

1 To be looked after.

2 Not to be separated from their parents unless it is for their own good, for example if their parents are harming them or not taking care of them.

3 If they are separated from one of their parents, to be able to stay in regular contact with them (unless they are likely to be harmed by doing so).

4 To give their opinion when a decision made by adults will affect them, and to have it taken seriously.

5 To be protected by the local authority from any harm arising from family breakdown or abuse within the family – though the local authority should not interfere unnecessarily.

6 To be removed by the local authority from a situation that social workers think is dangerous.

7 Not to have their privacy, family or home interfered with or attacked.

8 To be protected by society, wherever they are born and whether or not their parents are married.

9 To think what they like and to be whatever religion they want to be. To be helped by their parents to learn what is right and wrong.

10 To meet, make friends, and join clubs with other people, unless it interferes with the rights of others.

11 To have privacy, for example be able to write a diary that other people aren't allowed to see.

12 To be protected from abuse, violence and neglect and not to be hurt in any way, even by their own parents.

13 To have good health – this means to be taken care of and to have professional care and medicines when they are sick.

14 To have a good enough standard of living. Parents have the responsibility to make sure their children have food, clothes and a place to live. If parents can't afford this, the government should help.

15 To have free and compulsory education, at least at primary level.

16 To be able to access information from a variety of sources, and to be protected from harmful information.

17 To rest, play and enjoy leisure time.

Rights 7, 8 and 15 are adapted from the *Universal Declaration of Human Rights*; 5 and 6 are adapted from Social Services guidelines; and all the others are adapted from the *Convention on the Rights of the Child*.

Would you add any more suggestions to this list?

Who makes sure that young people get their rights?

A total of 191 countries had signed the *Convention on the Rights of the Child (CRC)* by 2001. Like the *Universal Declaration of Human Rights*, the *Convention* is not legally binding. However, the countries that sign these conventions, including the UK, are agreeing to put them into practice and are meant to make sure that all new laws fit with them. Every five years, the government has to write a report for the International Committee on the Rights of the Child about how they are making the CRC work in practice.

In 2002, the Children's Rights Alliance for England (CRAE), an alliance of many organisations working with young people, wrote a report highlighting areas where they thought children's human rights were not being upheld. Children's rights groups and organisations have an important role to play in raising awareness about the *Convention* and should refer to it whenever they make decisions affecting children. CRAE suggests that young people should quote the *Convention* whenever they contact their MP about an issue concerning children's rights.

Tasks

1 Make a list of the rights and responsibilities you have in your family.
2 Look at the possible rights suggested.
  a Divide them into three groups:
   • those you think should be legal rights
   • those you think are moral rights
   • those you think are not rights.
  b Which rights do you think are most important?
3 Read the list of rights. Write a corresponding list of responsibilities that these rights place on:
  a parents
  b local authorities
  c governments.

Discussion

Think about the following questions in preparation for a class discussion:
• Should there be universal rights for children?
• Should parents have to accept that their children have rights?
• Should children's rights have anything to do with age?
• Should children's rights have anything to do with gender?
• Who should be responsible for making sure that children's rights are respected within families?
• How can moral rights be ensured if they are not also legal rights?
• Do you have any role in ensuring that your rights are respected?
• Do you have any role in helping other children to have their rights respected?

Further information

For the full text of the *Universal Declaration of Human Rights*, see:
www.un.org/Overview/rights.html
For the full text of the *Convention on the Rights of the Child*, see: **www.unicef.org/crc/crc.htm**
This site also gives information on the origins and implementation of the *Convention*.

The right to education

Article 26

1 Everyone has the right to education. Education shall be free, at least in the elementary and fundamental stages.

2 Education shall be directed to the full development of the human personality and to the strengthening of respect for human rights and fundamental freedoms.

Universal Declaration of Human Rights

Read the information below, which illustrates how the government's role (and responsibilities) have increased over time to fulfil your right to education. Then answer the questions in the timeline.

Timeline of British education

1918
Schooling becomes compulsory up to the age of 14, and free in elementary schools. This is the first example of a free and compulsory system of state education.

1 Do you think a free education system is needed, or could the government charge us directly for schools?

1944
School-leaving age rises to 15. Universal free schooling in three different types of school, based on the strengths and interests of students. Which type of school a student goes to is based on how well they do in the 11+ examination.

PRIMARY EDUCATION

Secondary modern	Grammar	Technical
General, more vocational	More academic	Technical and vocational

2 Do you think different needs and interests are best catered for in separate schools like this, or in the same school with a variety of options?

1965
Growing numbers of **comprehensive schools** to provide for all abilities from the age of 11 up to 16 or 18. These schools are seen as another way of meeting the requirements of equality of opportunity and a suitable education for all.

3 Do you think comprehensive schools are a good way to create equality of opportunity in education?

1973
The school-leaving age is increased to 16 years of age.

4 Do you think the school-leaving age is right now? Should it be changed?

1979
Some people blame comprehensive schools for a decline in standards, and criticise their teaching techniques. There is growing pressure to return to more traditional teaching methods.

5 Who should determine the style of education provided for young people:
a young people? **b** teachers/schools?
c government?

1984–87
There is a long period of industrial action involving teacher strikes, resulting in new laws governing teachers' pay and conditions.

6 Should teachers have the same right to strike as other workers?

1986
Corporal punishment is banned in all state schools.

7 Should teachers be able to beat students who disrupt the learning of others?

1988
The Education Reform Act introduces a National Curriculum for schools. This defines what is to be taught in schools, and at what level.

8 Who should decide what is taught:
a young people? **b** employers?
c schools? **d** parents?
e the government?

1995
New qualifications are introduced to encourage a more vocational route for some students.

9 Do you think school does enough to prepare you for the world of work?

10 What changes would you make to ensure that young people's right to education is fulfilled?

Rights into reality

Case study: Summerhill School

Aims

Summerhill aims to provide choices and opportunities that allow children to develop at their own pace and to follow their own interests.

Summerhill does not aim to produce particular types of young people, with specific, assessed skills or knowledge, but does aim to provide an environment in which children can define who they are and what they want to be.

Activities

There is no 'average' day at Summerhill. The students define their own day. Most of the 91 children live at the school.

At 8:15 am the school is woken-up by elected 'Beddies Officers'.

A lesson bell rings at 9:30, and regularly through the day announcing further lessons. The older children choose the subjects they want to study at the start of each term. The younger children have their own class teacher and area, but do specialist lessons like science with trained staff.

On Tuesdays and Fridays, at 2 pm, the whole community holds democratic meetings to create rules, discuss issues and to raise problems like social problems, items being stolen, etc.

This all sounds a very structured day, yet the students decide if they want to go to lessons. Instead of going to class you can find them reading, making tree huts, playing in the sand pit, chatting, lying in the sun, surfing the web, playing games, etc.

On 23 March 2000, in the Royal Courts of Justice, Summerhill finally won its fight against school inspectors to recognise the right of its children to control their learning. The front page of *The Daily Telegraph* announced: 'Children win right to miss lessons'.

As one school leaver said:

'I have been relaxed, open minded and I have found my personality here, so people can see who I am and not what grades I get.'

Freedom of speech and information

Article 18

Everyone has the right to freedom of thought, conscience and religion; this right includes freedom to change one's religion or belief, and freedom, either alone or in community with others and in public or private, to manifest one's religion or belief in teaching, practice, worship and observance.

Article 19

Everyone has the right to freedom of opinion and expression; this right includes freedom to hold opinions without interference and to seek, receive and impart information and ideas through any media and regardless of frontiers.

Universal Declaration of Human Rights

Some rights are **absolute rights**, such as the right to life which cannot be denied. Others are **qualified rights** which may sometimes be limited when they have an impact on other rights. This section looks at the importance of the rights to freedom of speech and freedom of information, and at times when they may be limited.

▲ **Speakers' Corner is in Hyde Park, London. People have voiced their concerns there since 1872. Every Sunday, anyone can speak about any topic they like, so long as they are not obscene or blasphemous.**

Why are freedom of speech and freedom of information important?

Freedom of speech and freedom of information are two sides of the same principle. **Freedom of speech** involves being able to state your opinions and beliefs freely. **Freedom of information** involves being able to access the opinions of others freely, and also to access information about issues that are important to you.

Being able to think and say what you want, particularly about public issues that affect all our lives, is part of being human. In the UK, we are generally allowed to say what we want, although there are cases of people being silenced. In many countries, free speech is more limited, and criticising the political system or government can lead to extreme punishments. Many people in the countries of the former USSR say that there, one of the most important positive changes is that they are now free to speak their mind on a range of issues.

It is hard for people in Britain to imagine what it would be like to be afraid of saying anything critical about the government or government services in case someone overheard you and reported you.

Source A

The right to free speech is one of the most important and fundamental rights of liberty... The advent of the internet has seen a staggering growth in the potential for the freedom of speech and expression of people throughout the world. Sadly, in some quarters this same freedom is being abused and used irresponsibly as a smoke screen to communicate in a vulgar, profane, violent and insulting manner.

Dr Alan Keyes says 'Freedom requires that at the end of the day we accept the constraint that is required'.

adapted from: www.zondervan.com
a Christian publisher

SOURCE B

Mugabe outlaws opposition and bans free speech

Legislation that has been likened to the worst excesses of the apartheid era in South Africa will be pushed through Zimbabwe's Parliament this week, effectively outlawing President Robert Mugabe's political opponents and stifling free speech.

The new laws allow Zimbabwe's police to ban political gatherings at will and prosecute anyone who attends a meeting where the government is criticised. They effectively ban opposition political parties and end freedoms of association, speech and movement.

Peta Thornycroft in *The Daily Telegraph*, 19 December 2001

The Internet

Governments have often controlled their people by restricting their access to information. Lack of information about what is wrong and what could be better about their government prevents them from protesting against it. It is claimed that the internet means that everyone can have free access to information. However, 80% of the world's population live in developing countries yet they have only 8% of the total internet access. Only 1% of internet users are in Africa (for statistics on internet use, see: **www.nua.com**).

The internet does increase freedom of information but there are problems:
• It is difficult to restrict pornography and websites that incite people to violence.
• There is no guarantee that facts are accurate, unless you are using a very reputable website – you should always check facts that you read on the internet.

Provoking hatred and violence

Some people use the power of speech to provoke hatred and violence. In this case the right to life is considered more important than the right to free speech. It is not permitted to make racist public announcements that may lead people to violent actions. It is also not permitted to make public announcements recommending attacking people who are racist. In February 2002, the Council of Europe was considering a draft agreement that would require states to pass laws in their own countries in order to outlaw:

● offering or making available xenophobic (racist) material to the public through a computer system
● distributing racist or xenophobic material to the public through a computer system
● producing such material in a computer system for distribution to the public.

Tasks

1 Look at source A.
   a Do you agree that free speech needs limits?
   b Describe a situation in which you think people should have their freedom of speech limited.
2 What are the effects on politics if freedom of speech is too severely limited (see source B)?
3 What rules would you set on freedom of speech?
   a Can you think of any that would be appropriate for your classroom?
   b Would the same rules be acceptable for the whole of society?

Discussion

• Do you think Britain should agree to the Council of Europe agreement?

• Could such laws be implemented?

• Would this limit of people's freedom of speech be justifiable? Why/Why not?

Extension

Why do you think so many journalists are prepared to risk their lives to investigate events? You could carry out some research by using the following websites:
Digital Freedom Network: **www.dfn.org**
Index on Censorship: **www.indexonline.org**

Limiting freedom of information

State secrets

Certain aspects of national intelligence and defence would not work if everyone knew about them. The MI5 and MI6 government departments collect information through secret means; if everyone knew where a spy got their information from, they would probably lose that source of information. In a war, the army can only be successful if the enemy does not know what the army's plans are. Matters of intelligence and defence are, therefore, covered by the Official Secrets Act.

Exactly what type of information should be covered by the Official Secrets Act is an issue for debate. Some people argue that we vote for the government and pay taxes for services such as intelligence and defence, so we should know more about what is happening in these areas.

C
The fact that a vaccine that is in common use has a 0.0001% chance of causing brain disease

Public information – or secrets?

A
The code for firing a nuclear weapon

B
The names of the companies that tendered to buy a public water company

D
The cost of redecorating a minister's house (paid for by taxpayers)

E
Evidence that aliens have landed and are living amongst us

F
We have sent so many troops abroad, there are not enough left to defend us if anyone attacks the UK

G
A breakdown of MI5's budget

H
The movement of nuclear waste on trains around Britain

I
The total amount of money spent by the government every year

Tasks

1 Look at the statements A–I on this page. Which do you think should be secret and which should be public information?
2 Discuss your answers with others in the class.

Privacy *vs* Public interest

There are ongoing debates about what is private and what is in the public interest.

- Do we have a right to information about the private lives of public figures?
- Do we have a right to know where a politician had her hair cut?
- Do we have a right to know if a politician smoked cannabis 20 years ago?
- What about the spouses and children of celebrities?
- Do we have a right to know where a politician sends her child to school?
- Do we have a right to know where a politician sends his child to school if he is the Education Minister?

Celebrities

Is it in the public interest to know the details of singers' and actors' private lives?

If celebrities use the media to promote themselves, can they expect privacy when they want it?

Complaints

Obviously, many people are unhappy about what is written about them in the newspapers. Sometimes this is justified – the press does intrude on people's privacy. Complaints can be made to the Press Complaints Commission (**www.pcc.org.uk**). This is **self-regulatory**: in other words, it is run by the newspapers. They keep a check on themselves because they do not want anyone else to keep a check on them. You can look at past cases of complaints on the newspapers' websites.

Is our press as free as we think?

Obviously everything that happens in the world cannot appear in the newspapers. But who decides what *is* news? Terrible things that happen slowly over a period of time do not become news. 'Third World debt' has been blamed for the deaths of thousands, but it does not hit the news unless there is a particular event, such as a country saying it is unable to repay its debts, or famous people make statements about it. This can be described as 'slow news', and in fact is often more significant than the event-driven news that appears in the newspapers.

There is an important way of having power, called **agenda setting**. Whoever decides on the content of a debate has a lot of power over the conclusions that people reach. Newspapers and television stations can be seen as setting the agenda for debate.

Discussion

The Minister of Agriculture has been married for ten years. He started having an affair a year ago. A newspaper asked him about it and he denied everything. Later there was so much evidence about the affair that he had to admit that he had lied about it before. He said he lied because he didn't want to hurt his wife. His wife has now left him and he is about to marry his girlfriend. He is still Minister of Agriculture.

Which of the following do you agree with:

- It is important for the public to know about the affair.

- The affair is private and the public have no right to know about it.

- The public should know about the affair because people who have affairs are bad Ministers.

- The public should know about the affair because Ministers should never lie. If he lied about his private life, he will probably lie about public issues.

- The newspapers should find out all the details of the affair, for example how they met, where they went on holiday, etc.

- The newspapers should be able to take photos of the Minister with his girlfriend.

- The newspapers should be able to take photos of the Minister's wife crying.

Do we *all* have a right to privacy?

What does equality look like?

In the following four pages you will look at the right to equality and how that applies in the workplace. The right to equality sounds simple but in practice it is not always easy to guarantee. Women and men often end up in different types of job and have different rates of pay. People who support the idea of equality sometimes end up discriminating, without even meaning to. Equality is complicated, and not just because people do not understand how it works – there are different meanings to the term. Below are two meanings to think about.

Equality of outcome

At the extreme this would mean everyone achieves the same. If there was equality of outcome in the workplace we would expect to see the same number of men driving lorries as women. This is unlikely, but in other areas, such as education, equality of outcome might be more desirable. At the moment girls tend to do better in exams than boys, and certain ethnic groups achieve different levels of GCSE passes; for example, in one London borough 33% of white students recently got five or more A–Cs, but 56% of Indian students achieved the same grades, and only 18% of Caribbean students. Clearly here we are more likely to expect equality of outcome so that everyone achieves the same, regardless of their gender or ethnicity.

Equality of opportunity

This means everyone has the same chance of achieving. You might argue that it does not matter what people achieve – only that they are not unfairly held back because of their disability, race, gender or any other factor. As long as lorry companies do not discriminate, it does not matter that only 2% of lorry drivers are women. The point is, any woman can be a lorry driver if that is what she wants to do. Similarly, as long as everyone has the same opportunity to be educated, it does not matter what they achieve.

Sports equity

'Sports equity is about fairness in sport, equality of access, recognising inequalities and taking steps to address them. It is about changing the culture and structure of sport to ensure it becomes equally accessible to everyone in society.'

Sport England

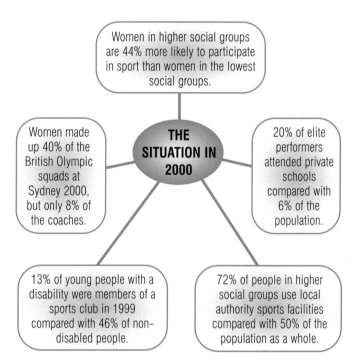

Active Sport is a major Sport England programme with the objectives of increasing participation in sport and reducing inequalities. It is a five-year programme targeting ten different sports.

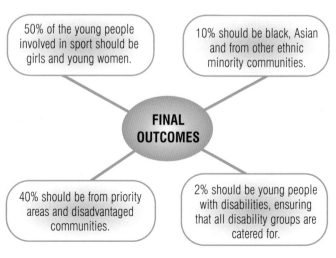

In America's Women's United Soccer Association (WUSA) league, in the first season of 2001, salaries up to $85,000 were on offer. In 2001, the Fédération Internationale de Football Association (FIFA) launched a wide-scale survey to find out how many footballers there are, worldwide. The results showed that there are approximately 250 million people who regularly play football around the world. Of that total, over 20 million are women footballers, 80% of whom are still in their teens.

Tasks

1 Which type of equality is most important in sport – equality of outcome or equality of opportunity?
2 Why do you think the inequalities in the top diagram opposite exist?
3 What obstacles will Sport England come up against in meeting its targets?
4 Why do you think women's football has not been as popular as men's football?
5 How do you think Abby (see 'Whistle Test') would manage refereeing in *your* school matches?
6 Is women's football encouraged in your school?

Whistle Test

In the United States, where all things cool come from as far as teenagers are concerned, 'soccer' is as much a woman's game as it is a man's, and female stars have achieved professional and even cult status with their progress in the women's World Cup.

When my daughter Abby was 14, she was slight, shy and reserved. But her pocket money was no longer funding her taste in clothes and CDs, so she set out to supplement her income with a weekend job. 'Why don't you take up football refereeing?' I suggested. After all, she had seen me vanish through the door every Sunday morning to take charge of local league matches (I'm a qualified referee). 'Dad, I'm only 14,' she protested. I told her that that was no problem as she would initially be given minor league matches involving teams under the age of 16.

After two months of pondering the implications, she announced at tea one evening that she was ready to take a 10-week FA course leading to a refereeing qualification. The result was a boost to her confidence – she took the group top mark of 87 per cent and was instantly presented with her refereeing credentials.

adapted from Alan Combes in the *Times Educational Supplement*, 14 December 2001

Debate

What would equality look like in football?
• Equal respect for women's football as a minority sport?
• Women and men playing in mixed teams?
• Women's football involving as many people as men's football?
• Women involved in local football?
• Women involved in international football?

Extension

Carry out your own survey about what sports young people in your school:
a participate in, and
b would like to participate in.
Do you have equality in sports in your school?

The right to equality

Article 1

All human beings are born free and equal in dignity and rights. They are endowed with reason and conscience and should act towards one another in a spirit of brotherhood.

Article 2

Everyone is entitled to all the rights and freedoms set forth in this Declaration, without distinction of any kind, such as race, colour, sex, language, religion, political or other opinion, national or social origin, property, birth or other status.

Universal Declaration of Human Rights

To ensure the right to equality, successive UK governments have introduced a range of legislation in the form of **acts**. The acts themselves are often long and complicated but brief outlines of some of the main ones are set out on this page. All acts, unless specifically stated, relate to equal opportunities in all areas of employment, education, the provision of goods, facilities and services, and in the management of premises.

Equal Pay Act 1970
This act gives individuals a right to the same pay and benefits as a person of the opposite sex in the same employment. The Equal Pay Act has been interpreted to cover indirect and direct sexual discrimination. Since the enforcement of this act, the pay gap between men and women has narrowed from 31% to 18%.

Sex Discrimination Act 1975
This act prohibits discrimination against individuals based on their gender. It also prohibits discrimination against people based on their marital status. Victimisation because someone has tried to exercise his or her rights under the Sexual Discrimination Act or Equal Pay Act is prohibited. The Sex Discrimination Act established the Equal Opportunities Commission to monitor that act and the Equal Pay Act.

Race Relations Act 1976
This act prohibits discrimination on racial grounds – meaning colour, nationality, ethnicity or race. The act established the Commission for Racial Equality to work towards the elimination of race discrimination. It does not apply in special cases such as the performing arts, where a particular character may need to be a certain colour, or in some social services jobs where employees need to work with specific ethnic communities.

Disability Discrimination Act 1995
This act prohibits unlawful discrimination against a disabled person in employment. Until October 2004, the act only applies to employers with 15 or more employees. The Disability Rights Commission was established under this act to monitor progress. This act is different from the previous ones because it requires employers to take positive steps to ensure equal access, for example to improve buildings to make them easier to use.

Employment Rights Act 1996
(and related regulations 1999)
This act gives people the right not to be unfairly dismissed – classed as reasons related to pay, childbirth, maternity leave, parental leave or time off to care for dependants. For example, it gives employees a right to maternity leave, a right to paid time off for antenatal care, and a right to unpaid time off when a dependant is ill.

Human Rights Act 1998
This act incorporates rights from the *European Convention of Human Rights* into UK law. Convention rights include a right not to be discriminated against.

National Minimum Wage Act 1998
This act ensures that workers are not paid less than a set minimum rate per hour.

Tasks

1 The National Minimum Wage Act 1998 requires that workers are paid a minimum hourly rate by law. Find out the following:
   a What is the national minimum hourly wage?
   b What types of job pay the minimum wage in your area?
2 In what ways do you think the minimum wage could help combat discrimination?
3 In what ways is a minimum wage not enough to guarantee equality in pay?

Research

With a partner or in a small group, find out more about one of the acts listed here. What does the act mean for our society – and what do you think would happen if it did not exist? Record your findings for the rest of the class.

Read the following examples and decide whether or not they are cases of discrimination. Use the summary of legislation opposite to help you decide.

A David is a computer programmer. He failed to get a job with a small company (with ten employees) as the manager felt he could not afford to make the changes necessary to make the building accessible for David's wheelchair.

B Some of the men at Mary's office are constantly making comments about her as she walks past them. Sometimes they ask her what she does in her spare time, or even try to guess what underwear she is wearing.

C Jan failed to get promotion even though she felt she was the best candidate for the job. The board have not told her the reason for her failure to get the job, but she suspects that they are concerned she may take maternity leave in the next few years. She has recently married and is keen to start a family.

D Abdul applied for a job as pub manager. He has some experience of working in pubs and felt he was qualified for the position. The company said they would be interested at a later date but did not feel it would be appropriate to ask him to work in this particular pub as the customers are mainly white, conservative, middle-aged men. The company is worried that an Asian landlord might have problems.

E Ian runs a small shoe shop in the city centre. He advertised for a sales assistant but specified that he did not want applicants from the East End of the city as in his experience they often have unemployed friends who hang around the shop and put off other customers. About 50% of the East End population are from ethnic minority groups, compared with an average of 5% for the whole city.

Discussion

A The Disability Discrimination Act is clear on this issue.
- How could you convince employers that the expense of adapting buildings is worth it?
- What would be a sensible limit on the expenditure required of such companies?
- Do you agree that companies that cannot be inclusive for disabled people should not be able to continue in business?
- If you are not disabled, do you think your answers would change if you developed a disability?

B The Sex Discrimination Act is clear on this issue.
- What do you think should happen to the men in this example?
- What do you think should happen to the company?
- What do you think might prevent people taking action under this legislation?
- Is it acceptable for a woman to make sexist jokes in the workplace?

C The Sex Discrimination Act is clear on this issue (even without the additional support of the Employment Rights Act).
- How easy do you think such a case would be to prove?
- What evidence would you look for in such a case?

D This case would not fall under the exemptions (special cases) of the Race Relations Act.
- Is it right to try to guess what problems might be created by customers' reactions to an employee?
- What action should the company have taken?
- Can you think of other examples where people might be tempted to discriminate, on the misunderstanding that they are trying to be fair?

E This case is different. It is **indirect discrimination** under the Race Relations Act. The effect of these decisions is to discriminate against people in the ethnic minority groups who are more likely to live in the East End.
- Can you think of other examples where indirect discrimination may occur against any group?

Equal rights, equal pay?

The United Kingdom has the widest gender pay gap of all the European Union states. The three main causes of unequal pay are:

1 sex discrimination in the pay system
2 more women being concentrated in low-paid jobs such as shop assistants, teachers, secretaries and nurses
3 women still taking prime responsibility for childcare, so many go into part-time jobs which are more likely to be badly paid.

Did you know?

- Women working full-time earned 19% less per hour than men working full-time in 1999.
- Women working part-time earned 13% less per week than men working part-time in 1999.
- Women's average weekly income was less than half of men's.
- Over a lifetime, the difference earned between a man and a woman is estimated at £250,000.

Women often do very different jobs from men:

	Percentage of workers	
	women	men
Lorry and van drivers	2	98
Chefs and cooks	50	50
Computer analysts/programmers	21	79
Secondary school teachers	53	47
Primary school teachers	86	14
Marketing and sales managers	29	71
Checkout workers	81	19
Nurses	90	10

EOC Analysis of Labour Force Survey (2000), Office for National Statistics

Maternity and paternity leave: who gets the best deal?

Maternity leave

A woman is entitled to 18 weeks' maternity leave. However, if she is to have the 18 weeks' maternity leave paid, she must have been employed for at least 26 weeks, including the 15 weeks before the baby is due. If all these conditions are met the woman can claim 90% of her normal wage for 6 weeks, and the statutory minimum from then on (£60.20 in 2000). If a woman has completed one year's service at her employment, she is entitled to additional maternity leave – which totals 29 weeks following giving birth.

SOURCE A

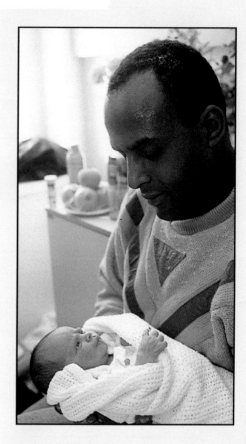

Britain has some of the weakest paternity leave and paternity pay rights in the western world. In Finland, fathers of newborn babies are entitled to 42 days' paid paternity leave; and the country's Prime Minister took paid paternity leave on the birth of his two daughters. In Brazil, fathers are entitled to five days' paid paternity leave.

British fathers have had to rely on individual company policies on paternity leave and informal arrangements with employers. A new measure was introduced on 15 December 1999 after the EU's Parental Leave Directive, allowing fathers to take 13 weeks' parental leave for each

adapted from Patrick Collinson in
The Guardian, 2 June 2001

Oh baby, it's a birth right

child under five years old. But because the legislation did not require employers to make any payments, the take-up of the new right has been lower than 2%.

A survey by bank Virgin One of 1,000 UK fathers found that 45% of young dads said financial constraints prevent them from taking paternity leave, while a further 23% said that work concerns stood in the way of taking leave. Only 1% of respondents in the Virgin survey said they would not take paternity leave because they feel that parenthood is a job for their wives.

The good news for hard-up parents is new legislation that will give fathers paid paternity leave of £100 per week for two weeks. The bad news is that the new benefit will not begin until 2003. The new right is expected to benefit an estimated 450,000 working fathers each year, and campaigners say that, even at the relatively low level, it will make a huge difference for low-income households.

Maternity pay is paid at the rate of 90% of earnings for the first six weeks, and 92% of that payment is funded by the government.

SOURCE B

Congratulations – and goodbye (in part)

The Maternity Alliance, which campaigns for pregnant women and new parents, normally takes 35 calls a month from women who believe they may have been chosen for redundancy because they are pregnant. In October that figure rose to 58. This backs up a common hunch among equality officers and employment rights campaigners that women are being illegally singled out for redundancy because they are pregnant or on maternity leave.

'Birth Rights', a report published by the National Association of Citizens Advice Bureaux (Nacab) earlier this year found that tens of thousands of women are still sacked illegally or threatened with dismissal simply because they are pregnant. Others are asked to resign or reduce

their hours, while many are denied their right to return to the same job after maternity leave.

The Equal Opportunities Commission reported that the perception of maternity leave as disruptive and costly is especially true 'for small companies which cannot afford to employ extra staff to cover this period. While the woman is away, others must carry her workload and it is often difficult to cover their functions.'

'Small employers are not evil men,' stresses Emmott. 'They've got a tough job, trying to balance the books. And if someone's to go, they may in all innocence think that a young woman, who's about to take time off anyway to go on maternity leave, is the fairest place to start.'

adapted from Siobhan Stirling in *The Guardian*, 23 January 2002

adapted from Siobhan Stirling in *The Guardian*, 23 January 2002

Tasks

Look at source A.
1 How does Britain compare with other countries in terms of paternity leave?
2 Why do many fathers not take paternity leave?
3 Will paternity payments solve the problem?

Look at source B.
4 In what ways are pregnant women treated unfairly in the workplace?
5 Are all types of company likely to treat women the same?

Developing your opinion

1 In what ways are men and women unequal at work?
2 What do you think individuals should do to ensure greater equality?
3 What should businesses do?
4 Do you think men and women will ever be equal at work? Explain your answer.

Discussion

How could gender equality in the workplace be further promoted? What policies would you promote if you were responsible for this area of government?

Think about the advantages and disadvantages of the following options, including who will have the responsibility for delivering such policies and what it will cost them.
• Raise the minimum wage.
• Provide free childcare.
• Increase maternity leave entitlements.
• Allow equal paternity leave for men.
• Encourage women into better-paid types of work.
• Raise the pay for public sector workers, where many women work (e.g. teachers and nurses).

Who pays?

Money is not everything in life but it does play a very significant part for most of us. A very important aspect of citizenship is the balance between what we provide for ourselves and what the government provides for us. Another way to think about this issue is to consider what rights we have to receive benefits from the government, and what responsibilities we have to provide for ourselves. Look at the three major expenses on these pages and think about the balance between rights and responsibilities, and about the practical decisions that you may have to make as you get older.

Government or personal responsibility?

A EDUCATION

Since 1998 most young people who go to university have had to pay towards their tuition fees, and are also likely to have to borrow money to pay for their food, rent, books, bills and other living costs. They only start to pay back these loans when they earn a certain amount of money (in 2002 approximately £16,000 per year). In 2002 it was estimated that students left university with an average debt of £12,000.

The government does not expect students from poorer families to pay their tuition fees, and (in 2000) only families earning more than £28,000 were expected to pay the whole fee of £1,025.

Opinion 1
In Scotland, students do not have to pay towards their fees. In the past, student grants were generous enough for students to live on without getting into debt. The government should pay all fees and provide a generous grant to cover the real cost of studying. This could be funded by an increase in income tax.

Opinion 2
According to the higher education Careers Services Unit, graduates earned 31% more than non-graduates. For 45 to 49-year-olds, the difference grows to 76%. The government should tax graduates at a higher rate and use this money to finance grants and fees.

Opinion 3
Graduates gain the benefits of their education through better jobs so they should also bear the costs of their education. As long as there is help for the poorest students, asking individuals and their families to support their education fees and living costs is fair as they will earn the money to repay the loans.

B HOUSING

Housing is one of the biggest expenses in most people's lives. Even if you do not buy a house yourself, the cost of paying rent is often the biggest single item of expenditure in people's regular budget. In the UK there is a mixture of housing types: some people live in private rented homes that are owned by other individuals, others rent from local authorities, some part-buy their homes with housing associations, and some buy their homes outright. Over time there has been a shift away from local authority housing to encourage other forms of renting or ownership. Many council houses and flats have been sold to residents, often at low prices, reflecting the amount of rent money that has been paid to the council over a number of years.

Opinion 1
Home ownership encourages people to look after themselves and also encourages them to look after their own home properly and respect the neighbourhood. Government should encourage people to buy their own homes and should only provide housing for those who are on a low income and need extra help.

Opinion 2
Having a decent home is a right for everyone. The government should therefore build more council housing and encourage all families, not just the poorest, to live in them.

Opinion 3
Housing is important but government does not have endless amounts of money to build and maintain housing. Government should encourage housing associations, which operate like charities, to set up more renting and shared ownership schemes. This would mean that people have help getting homes but the government is not directly involved.

C PENSIONS

As people live longer, they draw their pensions for longer, and this has caused some serious problems for individuals and government.

The state provides a pension for most people that depends on the number of years people have worked. In 2002 the basic pension payable by the state was £72.50 a week for an individual; additional payments can be made for partners, for those with disabilities or for those over 80 years of age. The government is increasingly concerned that as people live longer, the number of pensioners will grow so big, it will be difficult to keep paying their pensions.

In addition, people can make their own savings for a pension, for example a man who had saved a pension fund of £100,000 by the time he was 65 years of age might be able to buy an annual income of £8,950 for the rest of his life. The actual amounts vary over time but in the year 2000, a 25-year-old man who wanted an income of £200 per week in retirement would have to save £209 per month, every month, for the next 40 years. (Figures from *The Daily Telegraph*, 4 November 2000.)

Opinion 1
More elderly people are fit and healthy at 65 years of age and have many years of life ahead of them. People should have to work longer – perhaps the government should increase the retirement age so that everyone has more time paying into the system (through taxes) and less time taking out of it (in pensions).

Opinion 2
Many people have paid into the pension system expecting to retire at 65. It would be unfair to make them work longer. Young people today should pay more in tax so that the government can provide more generous pensions to elderly people; they should also be made to save for their own pensions.

Opinion 3
The government cannot help everyone all of the time. If people want to be comfortable in their old age they will have to save for themselves. The government should provide a minimum pension for those in poverty but should force everyone else with a high enough wage to save for their own pension throughout their lives.

Tasks

1 Work in small groups. Each group should read about *one* of the issues and discuss the three opinions.
2 Pick one of the opinions or come up with one of your own, and write down as many points in favour as the group can think of. Think about:
   a Who would be affected?
   b What would be the impact on different groups?
   c What are the alternative costs?
   d What seems fair?
   If possible, find out some further information by searching newspaper archives on the internet or contacting companies and campaign groups that are involved in each area.
3 Present your case to the rest of the class and use your presentation as the starting point for a class discussion for each issue.
4 For each issue, write down your own conclusion. Make sure you think about rights and responsibilities in each answer.

Extension

People's attitudes to these issues are likely to change depending on their overall political point of view, their own financial situation and their age. Write some simple questions to find out people's opinions about these issues and ask a range of people the same questions. Think about who to ask and what might influence their answers.

Consumer rights

Whilst there are no provisions in documents like the *Universal Declaration of Human Rights* to give rights to consumers or customers, domestic law gives rights to us when we buy products or services.

The act of buying something creates a kind of contract between us (the consumer) and them (the seller). Because we pay money we can expect certain basic standards, and if we do not get them, we can take our case to court.

Your rights when buying goods

- The goods have to match the description. So if the seller tells you something is solid gold, it should be solid gold and not gold plate.

- The goods must be of satisfactory quality and do what they are supposed to do: a CD player must play CDs, a jacket should not fall apart when you wear it. If a shop wants to sell goods that are soiled or faulty they must point out the problem to you before you make the purchase.

- They must also be fit for purpose, so if you buy hiking boots that fall apart when you walk in the countryside, you may take them back.

If you buy something that does not fulfil any of these criteria you may take the goods back to the shop. If there is a small fault, the shop should fix it. If the repair does not work or there is a major fault, you can demand a refund. Even if shops have signs up saying you may only have vouchers or replacement goods, you still have a legal right to demand your money back.

If the fault on the goods caused damage, for example a new washing machine spoilt your clothes, you should also be able to claim compensation for the damage.

Your rights when buying services

Obviously things are not quite the same when you pay someone to *do* something, rather than buy a product.

- You can expect a decent level of service: for example, if you ask a hairdresser for a perm, you should not expect your hair to be straight when they have finished.

- The service should also be carried out with reasonable skill and care, and should be completed in a reasonable time and for a reasonable price. You would have grounds for complaint if a hairdresser cut your ear because they were watching television as they cut your hair, or a builder charged you double for a job they had already quoted.

If things do not work out as expected, you have the same rights as when you pay for goods. If you did not receive the service you agreed to buy, you can demand a refund or compensation.

Points to remember

1 You do not need a receipt, although it is often the easiest way to prove where you bought the goods or services.

2 You do not have the right to a refund if you simply changed your mind or because something does not fit. Many shops give your money back, or exchange goods for vouchers, but they do not have to. They often do so as a good customer care policy, but it is not a legal requirement.

3 You are not protected if you buy through small ads or from friends. The law only affects official retailers.

4 The contract is between you and the retailer. You do not have to deal with the manufacturer. If products are faulty, it is the retailer's job to sort them out for you.

5 Retailers cannot get around the law by putting up signs saying they are not responsible or they do not offer refunds under any circumstances. Even sale goods (those that are not marked down because of a fault) carry the same rights.

Tasks

1 Compare your answers for the scenarios below with those of others in the class.
2 Do the public know enough about their rights?
3 How do you think buying goods from the internet might affect your rights?
4 What responsibilities do you think consumers have to match their rights?

Extension →

Find out about organisations that help consumers get their rights, and then produce a leaflet or guide to consumer rights.

Useful organisations
The small claims court (listed under 'County Court' in your local phone book)

Citizens Advice Bureau:
www.adviceguide.org.uk

Trading Standards:
www.tradingstandards.net

Consumers' Association:
www.which.co.uk

Consumer Gateway:
www.consumer.gov.uk

Look at the following situations that you might face if you return faulty goods to a shop. Decide what you would do in each case.

We'll send it back to the manufacturers – you should only have to wait eight weeks for it to come back.

We cannot refund your money on goods bought in the sale. You just take a risk that you get a bargain.

We'll give you a credit note which you can use to buy anything else in the shop, but our sign clearly says no refunds under any circumstances.

Have a replacement from our stock.

Waterproof? Sorry that's a wrong translation from the Chinese manufacturer. You can get in touch with them if you want to complain – it's nothing to do with me.

What gives us quality of life?

Quality of life refers to the things that tend to make people feel happy with their lives. These may include having close friends and family, feeling safe, having enough money to meet our needs, having green spaces nearby, or having time to do the things we want to do. **Standard of living** is the phrase usually used to express the amount of money or material possessions someone has, which may or may not contribute to quality of life, but is unlikely to include all the things we need to be happy.

Advertising images often imply that if we buy a particular product, it will give us quality of life, for example a brand of drink linked with having fun with friends, or a make of car linked with a beautiful companion, an empty road and wonderful scenery. However, many of the factors that contribute to quality of life are the result of decisions that we take as a community, for example whether we decide to spend taxes on creating and maintaining parks, and whether polluting or non-polluting forms of transport are encouraged.

Fast car and a mansion? It's a recipe for despair

A group of psychologists from the University of Newcastle, Australia interviewed 1,400 people about what they wanted and valued in life. They found that people who most valued fast cars, big houses and expensive clothes and who wanted to impress other people with their possessions were the least happy with their lives and were most likely to be depressed, angry and discontented.

adapted from Lorna Duckworth in *The Independent*, 4 July 2001

Read the statements below. Which of them fits most closely with your idea of a 'good' life?

> The typical American dream is to own a big house, a 3-car garage, 2.4 children and a dog! It should have a white picket fence and be in a clean, safe neighbourhood close to a good school.
> BECKY HUFFT, KENTUCKY, USA

> What makes people most happy in Senegal is to be able to educate, feed and house as many of their family as possible.
> SOULEYMANE DIOP, SENEGAL

> Almost every Finn expects to own a summerhouse, a boat and a sauna. Possessing them might not make them happy, but not having them might make them feel unsuccessful.
> ANNIKA LUMIKARI, TURKU, FINLAND

> For most adult Sierra Leonians, best quality of life is having money and all the good things money can buy. To do this, they get involved in illegal digging for diamonds, or cutting down the forests for planting coffee.
> SHEKU SYL KAMARA, FREETOWN, SIERRA LEONE

> All my life I wanted a Mercedes-Benz car. All my life I thought that once I had a Mercedes I'd be happy and content. And so one day I was able to buy one. But as soon as I drove it, I saw a larger one. I wanted that one immediately. That's when I realised something was wrong.
> KRISS AKABUSI, BRITISH ATHLETE

Measuring national success

The economic success of a country is usually measured by **Gross Domestic Product (GDP)**, which includes all the money that changes hands. Some people are now suggesting that GDP is not a good indicator of success, because it assumes that any economic activity is good, even if it damages quality of life, for example a factory that creates air pollution or a disaster that leads to huge insurance payouts. A group of non-governmental organisations (NGOs) have developed a new **Index of Sustainable Economic Welfare (ISEW)**, sometimes known as the 'Quality of Life Index', which takes account of things like the environment and human health as well as money.

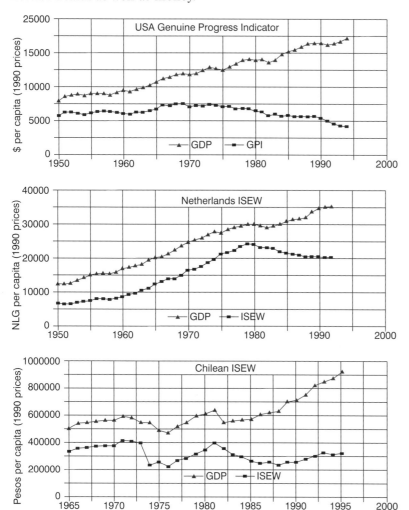

▲ Measuring progress by the Index of Sustainable Economic Welfare (ISEW)

It has been found that in the UK until the mid-1970s, as GDP rose so did the ISEW. However, since then, although GDP has continued to rise, the ISEW has begun to go down. Studies in Austria, Chile, Germany, Italy, the Netherlands, Sweden, Australia and the USA show similar patterns. It seems that increasing the wealth of a country does not always make its people happier. Part of this is due to increasing inequality between people. A small number of people getting a lot more money contributes to a higher GDP, but does not increase quality of life across the country.

Can your money change the world?

Can your savings change the world for the better (or worse)?

We are all encouraged to save money when we can – in order to buy presents, for a holiday, to go to college, for a deposit on a home or for our retirement. Naturally, we want to put that money where it will get a good return. But is that the only thing we should be thinking about when we decide which savings account to open or which pension plan to pay into?

When we put our money into a bank, building society or other financial organisation, it does not sit in a safe until we want it again. Instead, that money may be loaned to someone who needs a mortgage for a house or flat, or invested in a company wishing to develop their business. The company may be prospecting for oil in the Arctic Circle, developing renewable energy, making clothes or guns, selling cigarettes, or chopping down tropical rainforests to make garden furniture. Do you care what your money is used for?

More and more people do not want their money used in ways that go against their personal beliefs and principles. **Ethical investment** has developed so that people can have some choices about what their money is used for. It works in two ways. Some financial companies apply 'negative screening' – they decide on a list of things in which they will not invest customers' money, e.g. tobacco, nuclear power or animal testing. Others use 'positive screening' to support companies whose services are of benefit to the environment or to groups of people, e.g. fair trade, renewable energy, or education.

Is it any of your business what the bank does with your money? ▶

Can your spending change the world for the better (or worse)?

When you buy something, do you think about the effect its production had on the environment or on the people who produced it? Should you?

Buying locally produced food reduces energy use for refrigeration and transport, reduces the number of lorries on the roads, and contributes to slowing down climate change.

Buying low-energy electrical goods (from light bulbs to washing machines) contributes to slowing down climate change.

Buying fewer packaged goods and goods made from recycled materials (toilet paper, rubbish bags, etc.) saves energy and resources.

Buying fair trade goods (e.g. tea, chocolate, bananas) contributes to fairer wages and safer working conditions for people in developing countries.

Buying wood products with a Forest Stewardship Council (FSC) label ensures that they came from forests that are managed to maintain biodiversity and that tropical rainforests have not been cleared to provide them.

What matters to *you*?

Financial organisations offering ethical investment sometimes survey their customers to find out what kinds of things they do or do not want their money used for. Here are some of the criteria they may include.

We will not support companies that are involved with:

Human rights abuses
- denial of basic human rights
- working with oppressive governments

Arms trade
- manufacture or trade of torture equipment
- supplying arms to repressive governments

Manufacture of tobacco products

Ecological damage
- extraction of fossil fuels
- unsustainable harvesting of natural resources (e.g. deforestation)
- manufacture of environmentally damaging chemicals

Cruelty to animals
- blood sports
- fur trade
- animal testing of cosmetics and household goods
- intensive farming

Genetic modification (GM)
- reduction of biodiversity
- risks to food safety
- cloning
- domination of food production by a few companies

We will support:

Socially responsible companies
- fair trade
- fair treatment of workers, including those in developing countries
- charities, co-operatives and credit unions

Environmentally responsible companies
- renewable energy and energy efficiency
- recycling
- sustainable products and practices (e.g. forestry, organic or non-intensive farming)
- development of alternatives to animal testing

Tasks

1 In what ways could your spending choices affect other people or the environment?
2 Go through the list of ethical investment criteria and give each one a mark out of 5 (5 for strongly agree, 1 for strongly disagree). Compare your answers with those of others in your class. Are there other criteria you think should be included?

Discussion

Prepare for a discussion about ethical saving and spending with a group of other students or with the whole class. Think about:
- Is it our responsibility to be aware of the impact of our saving and spending, or should we be only concerned with meeting our own needs?
- What responsibilities do companies have? Should they be concerned about the impact of their business on the environment and about the employment conditions of people who work for the company in other countries, or are they only responsible for making the best profits for their investors?
- What might stop us from spending or saving ethically?
- What could companies or governments do to encourage us to spend or save ethically?

Be prepared to justify the ethical criteria that you have marked as important or unimportant.

Extension

To find out more about the criteria for fair trade products and for case studies of communities whose lives have been improved by fair trade, visit:
www.fairtrade.org.uk
- To find out more about the way the clothes we buy are produced, visit:
www.cleanclothes.org   Look for the price make-up of a sports shoe.
- To find more information about ethical investment issues, to read other people's opinions on them and contribute to the debate, visit:
www.co-operativebank.co.uk

Revision

Now that you have worked through Section 2, you should be able to answer the following short-answer questions. Once you have worked through the questions, check your answers with others in the class and with your teacher, and use the facts to start a set of revision cards. These can be completed as you work through other topic areas in your Citizenship Studies course.

A   Short answers

1   Give one example of an important event in human rights history.
2   Give one example of a **social right.**
3   Give one example of a **civil right**.
4   Give one example of a **political right**.
5   Name an international agreement that describes the rights that children should have.
6   Name one right that all children have.
7   Name one responsibility that is linked to that right.
8   Name one organisation in the UK that promotes children's rights.
9   Name one responsibility that each of the following has for children's welfare:
  a   schools
  b   parents
  c   local authorities
  d   central government.
10   List **three** groups that have responsibilities to provide education for all young people in the UK.
11   Give **one** example of legislation that gave young people legal rights to education.
12   List t**hree** pieces of UK legislation that support equal rights.
13   List **three** organisations that support equal rights in the UK.
14   Provide **one** example of the activities of each of these organisations.
15   Give **one** example of continuing inequality in the workplace.
16   Give one example of a **worker's right**.
17   Give one example of a **consumer's right**.
18   What is **ethical investment**?
19   What is **GDP**?
20   Give **one** disadvantage of using GDP to describe quality of life.

B   Source-based questions

Source A

'Each of us is responsible for everything and to every human being.'

Fyodor Dostoyevsky

Source B

'Where do human rights begin – in small places close to home – so close and so small that they cannot be seen on a map of the world.'   *Eleanor Roosevelt*

1   Give an example of how we are responsible for what happens to others.

2   Give an example of a 'small place' where human rights begin.

3   What message do sources A and B share in common?

4   What can 'ordinary' people do to promote and protect human rights in everyday life?

C   Extended answers

Write an essay on **one** of the following three topics. Remember to use evidence, and consider the issue from different viewpoints. You may express your own opinion in the conclusion.

1   Should there be a right to freedom of speech?
    In your answer refer to:
    • relevant rights in international agreements and UK law
    • other relevant rights that may conflict with the right to free speech
    • arguments for and against
    • practical examples where the right is limited.

2   'We will never achieve equality in the workplace.' Discuss.
    Consider the following:
    • what is meant by equality
    • the ways in which inequality exists today
    • the changes that have happened over time
    • the reasons for continued patterns of inequality.

3   Who is responsible for your human rights?
    • You   • Other individuals   • Organisations

D   Active ideas

You may choose to become involved in active experience relating to rights. The following are some ideas.

1   While on a work experience placement, carry out research into how the organisation promotes equality or health and safety.

2   Plan and carry out a 'Human Rights Day' in your school.

3   Join an organisation that campaigns for human rights, and do something to support its campaign.

4   Review the equal opportunities policy in your school. Make a presentation to governors and/or teachers about how it is being implemented, and how it could be improved in the future.

5   Carry out consultations with other students about how well human rights education is covered in your school.

How government works

In this section we look at the work of government – how it sets laws, how they are implemented, and the UK government's relationship with other governments around the world. Modern governments are very powerful and affect our lives in many ways, but in democracies ordinary people can influence governments too. As you read this section, think about who has power, and how citizens can influence those people in the exercise of that power.

The British state

This diagram shows some parts of the British state. We look at other parts later in this section.

ELEMENTS OF THE BRITISH STATE

GOVERNMENT	HOUSE OF COMMONS	HOUSE OF LORDS	THE MONARCHY
A select group of MPs, members of the House of Lords and others, are chosen by the Prime Minister to run government departments and make everyday decisions.	No law can be passed until members of the House of Commons have voted for it. The House can also bring down a government by passing a 'vote of no confidence'.	This part of Parliament mainly revises and advises the government on laws that are being passed. It can slow down laws it does not agree to, but the House of Commons has the power to pass any law, even if the Lords disagree.	The monarch (Her Majesty the Queen) still has some power but generally agrees to do what the elected government asks.

THE ROLE OF CITIZENS

Citizens can write to members of the government, lobby them and support the opposition. Some citizens are able to vote (or withhold their vote) in the next election for those government ministers who are MPs.	*Citizens elect every Member of Parliament. If they are disappointed with their MP they can elect another person to represent them, at the next general election. They can also demand to see their MP, and write to them about specific issues.*	*There are plans to elect some members to the House of Lords, but to date no-one has been elected to that House. Citizens can ask to meet individual Lords, write to them, and campaign on issues that the Lords are discussing. Some citizens are appointed to the Lords for personal outstanding achievement.*	*Citizens vote for the government which makes decisions about what the monarch will do.*

Tasks

1 Look at the information on these pages and make a list of the ways in which citizens can influence the actions of the state.
2 Which elements of the state can citizens vote for directly?
3 Look at those elements that are not in your list for (2). Do you think citizens should be able to vote for any of these directly?
4 Which elements of the diagram on these pages are involved with:
   a making laws?
   b shaping laws?

Extension →

What other methods are available for citizens to influence each of these areas of the state? Carry out some research to find other approaches and organisations that try to do this. (Section 4 and pages 60–61 in this section will be useful.)

ELEMENTS OF THE BRITISH STATE

THE PRIME MINISTER	THE POLICE	THE COURTS	THE CIVIL SERVICE
The Prime Minister represents the country, leads the strongest party in the House of Commons, selects the ministers and has power to influence policy in any department.	The police make decisions about how to implement the laws once they have been passed by Parliament.	The Courts interpret the law and decide what punishments are appropriate for those who break the law.	People are employed to translate government policy, laws and decisions into practice by delivering services to people.

THE ROLE OF CITIZENS

The Prime Minister is elected, like every MP, but becomes PM because he or she is elected to lead their party. Political parties make their own decisions about how to select their leaders. Any citizen can write to the PM.

Citizens can help the police when they are investigating crimes. They can also make their opinions known to the local police authority, which oversees the work of local police services and consults local communities.

Members of the public can serve on juries. They can also become magistrates, who judge the guilt of some offenders and decide on appropriate sentences.

Many citizens are civil servants. If people are unhappy about the services they receive, they can complain or take the relevant service to court. By doing this they can influence the way in which government decisions are interpreted and services are provided.

Government spending

The UK government collects money from citizens through individual taxes on earnings, sales taxes and through business taxes. In 2001/2 the amount of money collected by the government was £394 billion. It needs all this money to provide the wide range of services we expect from a modern government.

Every year the Chancellor of the Exchequer sets the budget, deciding on how much the government will spend and how it will raise this amount. As part of this process, ministers from other departments submit their requests for the money they think they will need to run their departments in the year ahead.

The following information shows how much the government spent in 2001/2. Imagine you are the Chancellor. Read through the following summaries of requests for additional finance. Which arguments do you find most convincing, and which would you ignore?

Transport:
£10 billion

Main areas: Responsible for investing in roads and railways

> For the last 20 years we have under-invested in transport. Our railways need repair and our roads are overcrowded. Transport delays cost the country billions in wasted working hours. A decent rail system is environmentally friendly and, in the long run, sorting out transport will save this country millions. We need another **£2 billion**.

Social Security:
£109 billion

Main areas: Responsible for making benefit payments including job seekers' allowance, pensions, child support, housing benefit and disability benefit

> The rich get richer and the poor get poorer. Raising benefits will help thousands out of poverty. We also need to raise child support, which will help to give every child a fair chance in life. By making sure everyone has enough money to live on, we are making huge savings elsewhere in terms of the costs of health, crime and other social problems. We desperately need an extra **£10 billion**.

Law and Order:
£23 billion

Main areas: Responsible for paying for the police force, probation service, the courts

> People don't feel safe any more. We need more police on the streets. Crime costs this country billions and it can ruin people's lives. Tackling crime must be the number one priority of any government, and it is popular with the voters. We need another **£5 billion** to get more bobbies back on the beat.

Health:
£72 billion

Main areas: Responsible for the NHS and promoting healthy living

> The NHS is falling apart. For years there has been serious under-funding. Doctors and nurses are underpaid. Buildings are crumbling and equipment is old. We need money to put this right and to cut the waiting lists. We also need to keep up with medical advances and to buy the latest equipment and medicines. Spending on health is always popular with the voters. We must have an extra **£7 billion**.

Housing/Environment:
£18 billion

Main areas: Responsible for the environment and improving the quality of housing

> We need to invest in renewing our inner cities, to regenerate deprived areas. Yes, this will cost money but in the long term we will all save when these communities are thriving once again. At the same time, we need to maintain and improve the countryside and promote a sustainable environment for all. To achieve these crucial aims we need another **£2 billion**.

Defence:
£22 billion

Main areas: Maintains the armed services: the Army, Navy and Air Force

> Our armed forces are overstretched. Peacekeeping duties around the world have increased enormously over the last ten years. If we want to have effective armed forces that can react rapidly to situations across the globe then we need to invest more in new equipment and personnel. In these troubled times we need another **£2 billion** to cope.

Education:
£50 billion

Main areas: Responsible for funding for schools, colleges, universities and adult education and training

> Teachers are overworked and underpaid, class sizes are too big, and schools need new buildings and equipment. Spending money on education will increase the wealth of all of us in the long run, as a new generation of scientists, engineers, programmers and creative artists emerge. Spending on education is always popular with the voters. To improve schools and invest in all our futures we need **£8 billion**.

Industry/Agriculture/Employment: £16 billion

Main areas: Helping to promote industry where required, helping farmers and fishermen produce safe food, and providing training for employment

> In other countries, industries receive far more help from government. If our industries are to compete on a global scale then they will need the right sort of help. Our farmers, too, desperately need support to cope in these troubled times. Helping in all these areas should increase overall employment and reduce the amount we spend on benefit payments. We need an extra **£2 billion** to safeguard jobs.

Debt interest and repayment:: £23 billion

Main areas: Repaying the interest and some of the capital the government previously borrowed

> The sooner we can pay off the national debt the better. Every year we are charged interest on the money we owe. If we can clear the debt then we won't have to make any more interest repayments. We must prioritise this area, as it will save money in the long run. We need an extra **£4 billion**.

Other smaller departments and items of government spending account for £51 billion. This includes the Foreign Office; culture, media and sport; and overseas aid.

Tasks

1 Which of these requests for more money do you think are the most important?
2 If you were Chancellor, how much additional money would you be prepared to provide to these areas of government?
3 Prepare a short speech justifying your decisions. As well as providing reasons for supporting some departments, explain your reasons for refusing others.
4 How do you think voters would respond to your choices?

Extension

Do some more research on how governments raise money. Which taxes do you think it would be best to raise in order to fund the further spending you have agreed to?

Influencing government

Lobbying is the term that is used when people try to influence MPs. It originally described the place where people would wait to talk to MPs, in the lobby outside the chamber of the House of Commons. Now the term is used to describe a whole range of actions that are designed to bring something to an MP's attention and to influence his or her opinion.

Individuals

Because MPs are supposed to represent everyone in their constituency, anyone can set up a meeting with their MP by arranging an appointment at the MP's surgery. You might want them to support you in changing government policy, to help you sort out a complaint that is not being dealt with properly, or simply to let them know what you think about an issue and to find out what they think. If you are successful, MPs can do the following:

- try to introduce amendments to draft laws (or even try to introduce new laws)
- ask questions about particular issues either in writing or verbally (all MPs' questions have to be answered by the government)
- follow up specific problems themselves (it is often easier to get decisions made and information provided if you can tell the person on the end of the phone that you are an MP).

As well as taking part in debates in the House of Commons chamber, MPs are members of committees that look into particular areas of government. Committees inspect draft laws in detail to make sure they will achieve their aims, they investigate issues that are felt to be important, and they also monitor the work of government departments. Members of the public can lobby committee members by:

- writing to or meeting with members of the committee
- sending in evidence for investigations by a particular committee
- suggesting new areas for future inquiries.

Charities and pressure groups

Some organisations use other methods to encourage an MP to introduce a new draft law, to ask questions in Parliament or to discuss issues with members of the government:

- **Petitions** – these can be good for making a point but also can be very easy to ignore.
- **Mass mail-ins** – these can be a very good way to get an issue noticed by an MP. Every MP receives hundreds of letters every week, but it does not take many – perhaps a few dozen – on the same issue to make them take notice.

- **Electronic campaigns** – sending mass e-mails can be quick and easy. It does, though, run the risk of annoying the MP or their office staff, who may have to wade through hundreds of messages before they can get on with their other work.
- **Briefings** – organisations can provide briefings on specific issues so that MPs are better able to get involved in debates. These can be in the form of sending information, or going to see individual MPs to talk to them and keep them up to date.
- **Professionals** – large charities often employ specialist lobbyists who monitor what is going on in Parliament, build relationships with friendly MPs and try to influence them over a period of time.

Company lobbying

Companies and businesses are also affected by decisions made by government. Rules and regulations about employment, health and safety, trading standards and taxation can mean millions of pounds to businesses. They often invest large sums of money trying to build special relationships with MPs and members of the government in order to protect their own interests. Some companies try to do this directly, while others use lobby firms and specialists to set up meetings. Lobby firms offer a range of services including:

- expert advice on Parliament and legislation currently being planned or discussed
- links to MPs and members of the government who have interests or experience in certain sectors of business
- planning for events at which meetings will occur.

For example, one company 'organised lunches and receptions arranged for business leaders ... to have private meetings with ... Cabinet Ministers, former Prime Ministers, the Queen's Principal Private Secretary ... and men at the very top of the UK diplomatic and civil service.'

from Lloyd Hughes Associates 1981 company profile, in Mark Hollinghurst's book
MPs for Hire: The Secret World of Political Lobbying, 1991

Tasks

1 What is 'lobbying'?
2 For each of the three groups described on these pages (individuals, charities and companies), explain why lobbying is important.
3 What advantages does lobbying have for MPs?
4 MPs have to register any payments or gifts they receive from any organisation outside of Parliament. Why do you think this is?

Some people worry that money buys influence. Others believe it can be a waste of time and money. Describing a typical meal set up by lobbyists, one journalist wrote:

'Go to a plush Westminster restaurant, on any weekday lunchtime, and you can play "spot the lobbyist". It is easy: pick out a Member of Parliament who looks well-fed but bored. He will be sharing a table with an industrialist who smiles rather too readily, and a PR man who seems well intentioned but slightly vacant. The industrialist will be flattered by the MP's attentions. The MP will be pleased to prove that there is indeed such a thing as a free lunch. And the PR man will take the profit from what will often have been an expensive waste of time.'

adapted from *The Economist*, 5 March 1988

Extension

Pick any controversial issue that has recently been, or is currently being, discussed in Parliament. The class should work in three groups (individuals, charities, companies). Each group must prepare to lobby an MP about the issue. One person in the class should take on the role of MP. Think about what each person or group would want the MP to do, and then present your ideas to the MP.
What decision did they make? Did you agree with it?

The Prime Minister

There is no single written constitution that sets out exactly what the relationships are between the different elements of the state. Many rules are scattered through different laws and traditions, and to a certain extent roles and relationships are therefore flexible. The Civil Service makes up the vast majority of those who carry out government decisions and duties, but the actual decisions are made by politicians. The balance of power between politicians in Parliament, the Government, and the Prime Minister, has changed over time but there is a basic relationship between them.

Prime Minister
The Prime Minister leads the government and his or her political party. The PM's main power is to choose Cabinet ministers and other members of the government and to oversee their work. The PM is always a member of the House of Commons.

Cabinet
These are senior members of the government who lead departments. They are all appointed by the PM and they meet regularly to update each other on what they are doing and to discuss important general issues. Most members are from the House of Commons but some are from the Lords.

Government
The Prime Minister chooses dozens of MPs from his or her own party to run parts of government departments. The PM can sack and appoint members of the government at any time. Members are drawn from either the House of Commons or the Lords.

Parliament
The leader of the party that has the majority (largest number) of MPs in the House of Commons becomes Prime Minister. Parliament is still the only institution that can pass laws. Members of the House of Commons question the PM every week.

What does the Prime Minister do?

Some of the main powers and duties of the Prime Minister are:
- meeting with the monarch once a week
- asking the monarch to dissolve Parliament and call an election
- appointing and dismissing ministers
- appointing the heads of MI5 and MI6 and senior appointments to the Church of England, the armed forces and the Civil Service
- calling and chairing Cabinet meetings
- overall responsibility for getting legislation through Parliament
- answering questions in the House of Commons
- overall operation of the Secret Services
- creating and changing government departments
- overseeing plans for emergencies and wars
- representing the UK at international meetings
- deciding on the use of armed forces
- launching a UK nuclear strike.

Although in some ways the role of the Prime Minister seems fairly limited, the PM gets involved in all areas of government and often discusses what is going on in departments in detail with the minister in charge. There is always a debate about whether a Prime Minister leads as an individual, like a President, or works more co-operatively with members of the Cabinet. Often the exact balance of power between a minister and the PM has more to do with personalities and abilities than set rules.

Tasks

1 What do you think are the Prime Minister's most important powers?
2 Read through the sources A–G below and make a list of arguments for and against the Prime Minister being powerful.
3 Why do you think Lord Hailsham (source F) thinks that being Prime Minister often leads to unhappiness?
4 What kind of person do you think would make a good Prime Minister?

Discussion

Who votes for the Prime Minister? Would it be better to have a directly elected President? Do some research into opinions on this issue and then hold a classroom discussion. Can you come to an agreement about which system would be best?

Source A

The office of the Prime Minister is what the holder chooses and is able to make of it.
H. H. Asquith, 1926: Prime Minister 1908–16

Source B

We have a system in which very great power is given to people if they have a large parliamentary majority ... The deal is that you give people very considerable power for five years, then they can be thrown out.
Lord Butler of Brockwell, 1998: Secretary of the Cabinet 1988–97

Source C

The Prime Minister is the chairman of a collective, which is called the Cabinet; and, once he has chosen his colleagues – and unless and until he fires them – his own strength lies essentially in being the Chairman of the Cabinet.
Lord Armstrong of Ilminster, 1999: Secretary of the Cabinet 1979–87

Source D

Number 10 is what the Prime Minister of the day makes it. The levers of power are all here ... The ability of the Prime Minister to use them depends on the Prime Minister being in touch with what is going on.
Harold Wilson, 1965: Prime Minister 1964–70, and 1974–76

Source E

A Prime Minister must remember he's only the first among equals... His voice will carry the greatest weight. But you can't ride roughshod over a Cabinet unless you do something very extraordinary.
Clement Attlee, 1961: Prime Minister 1945–51

Source F

I have known every Prime Minister to a greater or lesser extent since Balfour [who became PM in 1902] and most of them have died unhappy ... It doesn't lead to happiness.
Lord Hailsham: 1989

Source G

I'm worried about that young man. He's getting awfully bossy.
Margaret Thatcher, 1998: commenting about Tony Blair

Devolution

The United Kingdom is made up of four countries – England, Scotland, Northern Ireland and Wales. These countries came together gradually to form the UK. This process began with war and conquest, and gradually England consolidated its control through legislation. Laws were passed in 1536 and 1543 that made Wales part of England, Henry VIII became King of Ireland in 1541, and Scotland came under direct rule from London in 1701. For all of this time there was opposition to centralised London control; in Ireland it was particularly violent and eventually, after centuries of struggle, in 1921 the south of Ireland was recognised as a separate country (Eire, or the Republic of Ireland), but Northern Ireland remained part of the UK.

In Scotland and Wales, nationalists continued to call for independence, or at least a greater degree of authority to make decisions for themselves within the UK. These countries have strong identities which make them different from England, and the UK Parliament in London was seen by many as being more focused on English concerns, as most MPs represent English constituencies.

When Labour was elected to government in 1997 it introduced important reforms that would keep the UK together, but allow more decisions to be made in the different countries.

Giving more power to various levels of government outside of Westminster is called **devolution**. Following referenda (direct votes by citizens) in Northern Ireland, Scotland and Wales, when the majority of voters agreed with devolution, new parliaments were established that devolved power to the various countries that make up the UK.

Northern Ireland

69% of voters turned out for the first election in 1998.

Because of Northern Ireland's violent history and its deeply divided politics, there are a number of safeguards in place to make sure that all views are represented within the Northern Ireland Assembly and government. Although the First Minister was a Unionist, other ministers come from different political parties, e.g. for the first term the Education Minister was from Sinn Fein, a Republican Party that would normally oppose the Unionists.

The Northern Ireland Assembly has powers to pass laws in the following areas:

- Finance and personnel
- Farming
- Education
- Health
- Economic development
- Environment.

It can also pass laws in other areas, providing the UK Parliament agrees and that laws comply with the *European Convention on Human Rights*. As in Scotland, if there is confusion about whether power should lie with the Assembly or with Westminster, the matter must be resolved in court.

Tasks

1 Why do you think people in Scotland, Wales and Northern Ireland voted for devolution?
2 Scotland, Wales and Northern Ireland, as well as having representatives in their own new Parliaments and Assemblies, still elect MPs to be members of the UK government in Westminster. Why is this important for the UK?
3 England is now the only part of the UK without its own parliament. Would you vote 'yes' or 'no' in a referendum to establish an English Assembly? Why would you vote this way?

Discussion

Many people were worried that once devolution had happened it would create a new problem – Scottish MPs in Westminster would be able to vote on laws that only affect England, whereas Scottish laws would be almost completely set by Scots. The same would apply for Northern Ireland and Wales to a lesser extent.
- Does this matter?
- What could be done to avoid the problem?
- What would be the effect of any suggestions you come up with?

Scotland

59% of voters turned out for the first election in 1999.

No single party had a majority, so the Labour and Liberal Democrat Parties agreed to form a government together.

The Scottish Parliament has powers to pass or change laws in most areas of government including:

- Health
- Education
- Local government
- Housing
- Economic development
- Transport
- Criminal and civil law
- Farming and fishing
- Sports and arts.

The UK government in Westminster retains a range of other powers:
- Defence, foreign policy and the protection of borders
- Overall economic control
- Employment law.

In the first term the Scottish Parliament made several changes that showed it would not simply follow decisions made by the Westminster Parliament. It cancelled payment by students of tuition fees at university, and banned fox-hunting, both of which remained controversial in Westminster.

Wales

46% of voters turned out for the first election in 1999.

No single party had a majority but the Labour Party won 28 out of the 60 seats and so formed a minority government. This meant they had to rely on the opposition being divided if they were to win votes.

The Welsh National Assembly has fewer powers than the Scottish Parliament to make law. It generally exercises powers within broad frameworks provided by Westminster. This means that in areas such as education, the Welsh Assembly has the power to set its own curriculum. It can also decide which areas of Wales are classified as 'environmentally sensitive'. The legal status of the curriculum and of such environmental areas, though, is set by Westminster, and the Welsh Assembly cannot overturn or replace such laws.

New Labour, new local government

What does local government do?

Traditionally, local government has acted only in those areas that central government required it to. Since 2000 it has been possible for local government to take on a wider range of activities – as long as they promote the 'well-being' of people in the local area. This could mean that, in time, we will see differences emerging between local authorities in terms of what services they provide for local people. Despite this new flexibility, local government must continue to deliver many basic services, because they are required to do so by law. These services are described below.

Education
- Money from central government distributed to local schools
- Local advisers for schools, e.g. for Special Needs, Literacy, Numeracy, Ethnic Minority and Traveller Achievement Service (EMTAS)
- Recruitment and training of governors
- Youth Service

Housing
- Build and maintain council homes
- Administer housing benefit
- Work with housing associations to provide affordable local homes

Transport
- Maintain roads, bridges and pavements
- Monitor the services provided by local transport companies

Community Safety
- Street lighting
- Fire service
- Control noisy neighbours

Environmental Health
- Street cleaning and rubbish clearance
- Maintain parks and open spaces
- Food safety inspection for food shops and restaurants
- Local Agenda 21 to promote sustainable development

Social Services
- Children in care, fostering and adoption
- Support for mentally ill
- Residential care

Leisure
- Libraries
- Sports and leisure centres

Planning
- Give permission for all new buildings and significant conversions
- Draw up strategic plans for redeveloping whole areas

How should local government be run?

Councillors run local councils and are largely unpaid, being able to claim expenses only. Local people vote for councillors, and each councillor represents the people of one small area called a **ward**. In the past, councillors divided up into committees, each being responsible for one of the areas shown on the diagram opposite. For example, councillors interested in education issues or with relevant experience would sit on the Education Committee and elect a chair who would be their spokesperson. There is also a large permanent and paid staff who are employed by the council to carry out their policies and the various duties required by law.

The 2000 Local Government Act changed local government powers and introduced a new model for running local government. Every local area had to give up the old committee system, which involved all councillors, and choose between the following models:

Tasks

1 What model of local government do you think would be best?
2 If you were chosen as a member of the local Cabinet, what portfolio would you want, and why?
3 Would you like to stand as a candidate in a local election? Why/Why not?
4 These changes were introduced partly to make it clearer how local government works and who makes decisions. Do you think local people will be more likely to vote because of them?

1 Directly elected mayor with a Cabinet

2 Cabinet with a leader

3 Directly elected mayor with a Council Manager

Councillors selected for the Cabinet will have a **portfolio**. This makes them like members of the Cabinet in central government: they each have their own area, e.g. education, for which they are responsible. Like members of the central Cabinet they will also meet with other Cabinet colleagues to make decisions, work within the budget set for them, and present their decision to other councillors so that they can be questioned on these decisions.

All councillors still have a role in voting for the overall budget. They also select members of the Cabinet. Those without Cabinet responsibilities will carry out roles similar to those of MPs: they represent the interests of the people in their ward, and ask Cabinet members to justify their decisions and make suggestions to them. They also have to approve a constitution that sets out what the council does and how it makes decisions.

How is the law implemented?

Once laws have been passed, they need to be implemented. The police and courts are central to implementing and safeguarding laws. Often they shape the actual meaning of the law by the way they interpret it in their everyday work.

The Police and Criminal Evidence Act (PACE), which was introduced in 1984, contains most of the law setting out police powers and duties in all stages of the investigative process, from crime to trial. The PACE Act is aimed at striking a balance between police powers and the rights of the suspect. Under the Act, the Home Secretary is required to issue Codes of Practice, which give instructions on how these police powers should be exercised on a day-to-day basis.

The law and the Codes of Practice govern the police forces' day-to-day operations. The police service functions as an arm of the government – but how long do you think the arm of the law really is when it comes to shaping the laws in everyday situations?

The **Codes of Practice** cover five areas central to police work:

1 the exercise by police officers of statutory powers of stop and search
2 the searching of premises by police officers and the seizure of property found by police officers on persons or premises
3 the detention, treatment and questioning of persons by police officers
4 the identification of persons by police officers
5 the tape recording of interviews of persons suspected of the commission of criminal offences which are held by police officers at police stations.

Case study 1

1 It is a criminal offence to drive through a red traffic light.

2 The police have the power to pull over any person who does so and obtain the name and address of the driver. As it is an illegal action, a summons can be sent to the given address requesting the presence of the driver in court. If the driver is found guilty, they will receive a punishment and a criminal record.

3 The police officer has the discretion to give the driver a verbal warning and send them on their way.

Tasks

1 You drive through a red light and so does your friend on the same day at the same place. You receive a court summons, but your friend receives a verbal warning. How do you feel about that?
2 What reasons do you think might make a police officer give a driver a verbal warning rather than a court summons?
3 Do you think that breaches of the law should be dealt with in the same way by all police officers?

Case study 2

There has been much debate about the best approach to soft drugs in the UK. In July 2001 the police in the London Borough of Lambeth began a controversial scheme in which those caught in possession of small amounts of cannabis would no longer be arrested or prosecuted, but given a verbal warning and the drugs confiscated. The law still stated that cannabis was a Class B drug, and the sentence for possession was 5 years' imprisonment and/or a fine, and 14 years and/or a fine for supply.

Read through the following opinions on this.

SOURCE A

An internal review conducted by senior officers at Scotland Yard concluded that over the first six months of the scheme, 1,400 man hours were freed up. The number of seizures of cannabis rose by a third while seizures of class A drugs rose by 19%.

from Tony Thompson, 'Two countries took the drug test. Who passed?'
The Observer, 24 February 2002

SOURCE B

The reclassification of soft drugs such as cannabis is a ploy to reduce the administrative duties of police officers, with no consideration for the health and well-being of users.

Ian Burrell, 'Softly softly scheme on soft drugs lets off hundreds with caution',
The Independent, 3 January 2002

SOURCE C

60% believe cannabis should no longer be treated as a criminal offence. Up to 50% of young people try drugs. 2.5 million users were recorded in 2001.

adapted from an opinion poll, early 2002

SOURCE D

The new police tactic in the London Borough of Lambeth has been supported by the Metropolitan Police and coincided with plans by David Blunkett, the Home Secretary, to reclassify certain drugs:

The Home Secretary underlined the Government's determination to combat the scourge of Class A drugs such as heroin and cocaine. David Blunkett stressed the need to warn young people that all drugs, including cannabis, are dangerous. But he said there was a clear need to focus more effectively on hard drugs that cause the most harm and to get people into treatment.
Among other things he proposed to seek advice from scientists and medical experts on their assessment of arguments for reclassifying cannabis from Class B to Class C. He stressed that reclassification is quite different from decriminalisation or legislation. Cannabis would remain a controlled drug and using it would be a criminal offence.

Home Office Press Release, 25 October 2001

Tasks

4 Looking at the information in case study 2, give reasons why the scheme in Lambeth should or should not be developed throughout the rest of Britain.

5 List the differences you think reclassifying cannabis from Class B to Class C might make in Britain in relation to:
 a the police force
 b the public
 c the courts.

6 Do you think it is good for the police to have a level of discretion over how they implement the current laws on the possession of cannabis?

Extension

Do some research to find out what are the current laws on possessing cannabis. What is likely to happen to people in your area if they are found to be carrying it?

The right to party?

The debate over the Criminal Justice and Public Order Act (1994)

Laws give shape and meaning to our rights in relation to the state and to each other. Some laws are therefore likely to be controversial, especially where some people feel their rights and interests are directly affected.

The 1994 Act had an impact on many areas of activity. It introduced new restrictions and police powers in relation to squatting, public meetings and 'raving'. It gave the police more powers to stop and search people in areas where they suspected criminal activity, and also introduced the concept that any suspect who exercised his or her right to silence under questioning, could have their silence interpreted in court as evidence against them. Among other things, these powers were intended to make it easier for police to tackle trespassers who took over buildings and fields to organise illegal parties, or raves. Stopping and searching people would also help to deter criminals and catch people with illegal drugs who often attended such raves.

Sections 63, 64, 65: Raves

The Act defines a 'rave' as a gathering of 100+ people, at which amplified music 'wholly or predominantly characterised by the emission of a succession of repetitive beats' is played which is likely to cause serious distress to the local community, in the open air and at night.

The police have the power to order people to leave the land if they believe:
- they are preparing to hold a rave (two or more people)
- waiting for a rave to start (ten or more people)
- actually attending a rave (ten or more people).

Ignoring this direction, or returning to the land within the next week, are both offences, liable to 3 months' imprisonment and/or a fine of £2,500.

This law had support from groups of farmers who had found people trespassing on their land, and from local residents disturbed by raves. On the other hand it was controversial for some travellers, who felt their right to stop on land would be threatened. Squatters were concerned that their rights to stay in empty buildings would be threatened, and many people felt it was unjust simply because it removed their 'right to party.'

Tasks

1 Write down all the reasons you can think of for the introduction of the 1994 Act.
2 Do you think the law should be involved in stopping raves from happening?
3 Do you think people really have a 'right to party'?
4 Should the crime of trespass be treated in the same way, whether a group of people trespass in a field on a large farm or in a householder's back garden? Explain your answer.

SOURCE A

As party-goers we believe that it is the responsibility of the individual to look after themselves as grown and educated adults. We choose to make our own choices. We choose the right to party and free ourselves through dance and music.

from: www.partyvibe.com

SOURCE B

Farm leaders are calling on police to deal more effectively with illegal raves after two farmers were prevented from removing party-goers from their properties. Police arrested an Essex farmer on Boxing Day when he tried to confront ravers who took over his barn for a party.

Police said the 40-year-old Essex farmer was arrested to prevent a public order disturbance.

A National Farmers' Union spokeswoman said: 'Where farmers are suffering from illegal raves we would urge the police to effectively police these events. It would seem an extraordinary way to deal with the situation.'

An Essex police spokesman said police found up to 70 ravers in the barn at midnight being 'confronted verbally by the barn owner. After repeated attempts to calm the situation the officer arrested him in the interests of public safety.'

In response to criticism the police said: 'The Act only applies to raves held in the open air; this one was held in a barn. The law also states that there must be more than 100 people in the open air, causing a public disruption.'

Chief Superintendent Kevin Morris said: 'You have to use your common sense and ask what could a group of officers realistically do? You'd need 200 officers to deal with 100 revellers if they didn't want to leave.'

An organiser of the rave, who did not wish to be named, said: 'If the council were to give us a barn out of the way, we would use it – we would even go as far as to pay for it.'

adapted from BBC News articles, 3 and 4 January 2002

SOURCE C

Our reporter reports back on his recent involvement with Advance Party. Unfortunately he's had to be a tad skimpy on the finer details as we don't want to give you-know-who any unnecessary leads...

'The first thing to hit me upon meeting the organisers is their dedication to the cause of partying. For these people, the Criminal Justice Act made the illegal parties a very political affair.

One thing I was very impressed with was the reasoning behind some of the buildings chosen. With the Parkway cinema, a building that had been closed for three years after being bought by property developers (very useful for the local community eh?), the squatters staged film shows for local children and repaired damage to the building. Needless to say, after their eviction the cinema once again fell back into disrepair.'

adapted from: www.urban75.com

Tasks

5 What reasons might the squatters in source C give for using the old cinema for their own purposes (including raves)?

6 Why did the police not stop the rave in source B?

7 Why did the police arrest the farmer in source B?

8 In source B, which offence do you think was more serious – that of the farmer, or of the ravers?

9 What problems does the criminal justice system face in controlling raves?

10 Bearing in mind the experiences of the police, the land owners and the ravers, what amendments would you make to the law?

The justice system

Once the police have charged someone with committing a crime, there are several routes through the court system. These pages will introduce you to some of the key people and concepts.

THE LAW

Criminal Law: refers to behaviour that is forbidden by the state as generally harmful to individuals or the community. Criminal matters are dealt with in the Magistrates' Court, while more serious cases go to the Crown Court.

Civil Law: covers all areas of the law that are not criminal. Examples include family law such as divorce, education law and property law. It is the law concerned with private individuals and their rights and duties towards other private individuals. Civil law cases are held in the County Court or High Court. The Magistrates' Court deals with aspects of family law.

▼ **This is the common image of a court for most people, but only 5% of cases go to the Crown Court**

THE PEOPLE

Barrister: The main role of a barrister is one of advocacy – in other words, to represent people in court. Barristers also give specialist advice to solicitors.

Lawyer: This general term describes any member of the legal profession.

Solicitor: Members of the public go directly to solicitors for help with a range of needs, e.g. drawing up wills, property deals and divorce cases. Solicitors also represent clients in the Magistrates' Court.

Magistrate: A member of the public who is appointed to hear cases. Magistrates are not qualified in the law, so they have experts to advise them. Their job is to hear the case, decide on guilt or innocence based on the evidence, and pass an appropriate sentence. Normally three magistrates hear each case.

Judge: A senior lawyer in charge of trials that happen outside of the Magistrates' Court. In a civil trial the judge makes the judgement, and decides what the penalties or punishments are. In a criminal trial the jury decides on guilt and the judge decides the sentence.

Jury: Twelve members of the public who are chosen at random to decide whether someone accused of a crime is guilty or not. Anyone aged between 18 and 70 years can be called to serve on a jury, and it is an offence not to attend if called, although there are certain exemptions including police, criminals and those in the medical profession.

THE PLACE

Magistrates' Court: Over 95% of cases are heard in a Magistrates' Court. These cases include those involving young people and the least serious offences. 'Either way offences', such as theft, burglary and malicious wounding, are also heard by a magistrate, who decides whether they should be sent to the Crown Court. There is no jury in a Magistrates' Court.

Crown Court: A judge and jury hear the more serious criminal cases that are not dealt with in the Magistrates' Court. Very serious cases are tried here, such as murder, manslaughter, rape and robbery. The Crown Court can pass much heavier sentences than the Magistrates' Court.

County Court: Here a judge deals with smaller civil cases such as divorce and minor consumer disputes.

High Court: This is a more senior civil court that deals with more serious claims, where a judgement is needed.

Appeal Court: A judge hears appeals against the decision of a lower court. Appeals against the decision of the Court of Appeal go to the House of Lords, which is the highest court in the country. This system is designed to ensure that wrong judgements can be changed under certain circumstances.

COMMON CRIMES AND SENTENCING
(maximum term)

Theft: A person is guilty of theft if he or she dishonestly takes property belonging to another with the intention of keeping it. (*10 years maximum*)

Robbery: A person is guilty of robbery if he or she steals and uses, or threatens to use, force on anyone else. (*Maximum sentence – life*)

Burglary: Burglary is similar to robbery, but involves trespassing on another's property or home. (*Maximum sentence 14 years; or life for more serious offences*)

Murder: There are usually fewer than 200 murder convictions per year. Murder means illegally taking someone's life with the *intention* to kill or cause grievous bodily harm. (*Mandatory life – a life sentence has to be given for murder*)

Manslaughter: Killing someone without the intention required for murder. All unlawful killing, other than murder, is classed as manslaughter, e.g. causing death by reckless driving. (*Maximum: life; minimum: no imprisonment*)

Assaults and woundings:

- *Common assault* – between individuals, police intervene only to prevent a breach of the peace.

- *Aggravated assault* – this is a more serious version of common assault involving violence used upon a boy under 14, or any female.

- *Actual bodily harm (ABH)* – an assault that interferes with the health and comfort of the victim.

- *Grievous bodily harm (GBH)* – unlawful and malicious wounding.

Tasks

1 Under what circumstances do people without legal qualifications decide on a defendant's guilt or innocence? Why?
2 Why is it important to have an Appeal Court?
3 The police have charged Fred with murder. He plans to plead 'not guilty' and he knows he will have to go to court for a trial.
   a What court will he go to?
   b Who will decide his guilt or innocence?
   c What sentence will he receive if he is found guilty?
   d Who will pass the sentence?
4 Look at the cases below and decide whether they are likely to be civil or criminal cases:
   a shoplifting
   b consumer complaints
   c adopting a child
   d damage to property
   e disorderly behaviour
   f drunk driving
   g possession of a firearm.

Punishments

With every court case there must be a verdict, and for every guilty verdict a sentence must be passed. When a defendant is found guilty in either a Crown Court or a Magistrates' Court, the judge or magistrates will pass sentence, taking into account the circumstances surrounding the case, and any previous convictions. The background of the defendant may be considered too, if that is thought to have a bearing on the case.

Court sentences

1 Prison sentence

Life – is a minimum of 20 years.

Consecutive – a prison sentence which runs after another. For example, two consecutive sentences of six months are equal to twelve months in gaol.

Concurrent – a prison sentence which runs alongside another. For example, two concurrent sentences of six months are equal to six months in gaol.

2 Fine – the maximum limit in Britain is usually around £2,000.

3 Discharge – release.

Conditional – means that the charge will only be taken into account if there is a re-offence.

Absolute – means that there will be no criminal record.

4 Probation order – involves the supervision of offenders in the community. It requires an offender to maintain regular contact with police and probation officers.

5 Suspended sentence – a sentence can be suspended for a set period. If a re-offence occurs during that period, the sentence will be added on to the sentence for the new offence.

6 Community service – requires the offender to work between 40 and 240 hours of unpaid service, which has to be completed within 12 months.

Young offenders

A child under the age of 10 cannot be charged with a crime. Above this age, a criminal offence is considered to be a punishable act. In the 1990s more than 5,000 young offenders in England and Wales were held in institutions.

On a local level, Youth Offending Teams (YOT) bring together staff from the police, probation, education, health and social services, who meet to consider what they can do to help individual young offenders aged between 10 and 17. On a national level, the Youth Justice Board for England and Wales monitors the performance and operation of the youth justice system as a whole, including the YOTs, the youth court and the delivery of secure accommodation for young offenders.

The Act also included new powers for the police and courts to intervene when young people do offend.

Tasks

1 Read the three cases opposite. Imagine you are one of the magistrates in a youth court. Which sentence would you choose for the defendant, and why?
2 Do you think the sentences you gave would prevent the defendant from re-offending? Explain your answer.
3 How do you think your decisions would be interpreted by:
   a the young offender?
   b the victim of the crime?
   c friends of the young offender?

Final warning scheme
A first offence will result in a young person being given a reprimand. A further offence will lead to a warning or a charge. An offender may only be reprimanded once.

Detention and training order
Detention in secure accommodation where training takes place, followed by supervision in the local community by a member of the YOT.

Reparation order
This means that the young person must make amends to their victim or their community, usually through some form of unpaid work to benefit the community.

CRIME AND DISORDER ACT 1998

Action plan order
This includes a mixture of requirements in addition to being supervised, such as having to do unpaid work and having to stay away from particular places, e.g. football grounds.

Court ordered secure remand
Certain alleged offenders are sent to local authority secure accommodation.

Parenting order
The parent is ordered to attend counselling and guidance sessions to help them deal with their children, and must fulfil such requirements as the courts consider necessary, e.g. ensure school attendance.

Case 1

Dave is 14 years old and was excluded from his last school for bullying nine months ago. He has been unable to find another school and has limited literacy and numeracy skills. Dave lives with his father, who has a history of domestic violence, and with his brother. Both family members have been unemployed for six years since the closure of the local docks. Dave has been found guilty of burglary and resisting arrest. Dave was under the influence of drink and drugs when he was picked up, and told the court that he cannot remember becoming abusive to the police officer.

Case 2

Tommy is 17 years old and has been unemployed since he left school a year ago. He has been found guilty of taking and driving away a motor vehicle. He has two previous convictions for the same offence. He told the court that he only took the car for a laugh and that he is soon to become a father for the first time. Car theft has become a major concern in the local area and there is a growing local opinion that youngsters are getting away with it.

Case 3

Two 16-year-old boys and a 15-year-old girl attacked a middle-aged woman as she walked home from work. They knocked her to the ground and kicked her before stealing her handbag. The woman suffered severe bruising and a broken wrist. None of the teenagers has a previous conviction and they could offer no explanation to the court for their behaviour.

Discussion

'We should do everything to avoid sending young people to prison.' Do you agree?

The courts and human rights

In 1949 the UK government signed up to the *European Convention on Human Rights*. This meant that UK citizens had access to their rights, but they had to go to the European Court of Human Rights in Strasbourg in order to do so. In 1998, the UK Parliament passed a new law, the Human Rights Act (HRA), which made these rights part of British law, so that citizens can now claim the same rights in British courts.

Your Convention rights

Article 2 Right to life
You have the right to have your life protected by the law. The only exceptions are if the police kill someone accidentally in trying to maintain the law, e.g. in a riot situation.

Article 3 Prohibition of torture
You have the right not to be tortured or to suffer degrading treatment.

Article 4 Prohibition of slavery and forced labour
You have the right not to be enslaved or forced to work. Exceptions to this article include forced labour as part of a prison sentence, and compulsory military service.

Article 5 Right to liberty and security
You have the right to freedom and security. The state can deprive you of this right by arrest and detention if you break the law, or are suspected of breaking it. In such cases you have the right to an effective legal system in which you are tried in court.

Article 6 Right to a fair trial
Everyone accused of committing a criminal offence has the right to a fair and public hearing in an independent court. Everyone should be presumed innocent until proved guilty. You also have the right to defend yourself or to appoint others to do so.

Article 7 No punishment without law
No-one can be prosecuted for an act that was not illegal at the time it was committed, even though the law may have changed to make such an act illegal now.

Article 8 Right to respect for private and family life
You have the right to respect for your private and family life, your home and correspondence. This right can be limited in some circumstances.

Article 9 Freedom of thought, conscience and religion
You have the right to hold a wide range of views and religious beliefs and to act on them in public. This right can be limited to protect public safety and order, and to protect others' rights.

Article 10 Freedom of expression
You have the right to freedom of expression, including holding opinions and sharing information with others. Limitations can be placed on this right in the interests of public safety, national security, to protect people's reputation, and some other conditions.

Article 11 Freedom of assembly and association
You have the right to meet with others and join groups, including trade unions. Some exceptions may be allowed to protect public safety, for example the government can restrict the rights of the police or members of the armed forces to join a union.

Article 12 Right to marry
Men and women have the right to marry and start a family, according to the rights of the country.

Article 14 Prohibition of discrimination
You have access to these rights regardless of your sex, race, colour, language, religion, political or other opinion, national or social origin or other status.

Additional protocols have been added:
Protocol 1
Article 1 Protection of property
Article 2 Right to education
Article 3 Right to free elections

Protocol 6
Article 1 Abolition of the death penalty

Courts

The job of the courts is to interpret the Human Rights Act. It can do this in two ways:

1 Laws
Courts cannot overrule Parliament, and Parliament can still decide to pass a law that contradicts part of the HRA. However, governments in Northern Ireland, Wales and Scotland do not have this power and so the courts can overrule them if they decide that laws do not fulfil the requirements of the HRA.

2 Public services
The HRA only affects government and the services carried out by, or on behalf of, government. The

National Health Service, education system, Social Security and other similar services are all supposed to promote our rights under the HRA. This means that if you think your rights are being infringed by the way in which services are provided, you can ask the courts to make a judgement.

The following examples illustrate some of the ways in which these rights have been interpreted, and look at some of the issues.

Example 1, Article 14

This article is not absolute, which means that governments can discriminate in pursuit of other aims.

(a) New Deal is a government initiative aimed at getting young people aged 18-24 years into work. The government has taken legal advice and believes it is legitimate to offer services only to this group because it wants to tackle the specific problem of youth unemployment.

(b) Universities are also allowed to continue to discriminate against people on the basis of their academic ability, even though this excludes many people.

Tasks

1 Do you agree that discrimination in these cases is justified?
2 How would you feel if you were unemployed and 26 years old, and unable to get the support offered by New Deal?
3 Can you think of any other situations in which discrimination might be allowed?

Example 2, Article 12

The government can set laws which define and shape the extent of this right.

(a) Some religions allow polygamy - that is, men marrying more than one woman. This is not accepted as a legal marriage in the UK.

(b) Some gay and lesbian couples live together for years, share a mortgage and bring up children. Under UK law these relationships are not recognised as marriages.

Tasks

4 Should the law exclude these relationships from being recognised as marriages?
5 How might case (a) conflict with Article 14?

Example 3, Protocol 1 Article 2

This right is qualified because it has to be linked to the amount of money authorities have available to spend on the education service.

A schoolgirl with a mobility disorder could not get access to the room where her classmates worked, or the library, because they were both on the first floor. Her school arranged for her class to swap rooms with another, so they came to the ground floor and organised books to be brought downstairs for library lessons. Because she still could not have access to the science laboratories, which were located upstairs, she claimed that her right to an education was being denied. During the case the local authority said that a lift would cost £43,000, and the court ruled that given the financial restrictions, the authority was not in breach of the girl's rights.

Tasks

6 Do you agree with this judgement?
7 How much do you think would have been a 'reasonable cost'?

Example 4, Protocol 1 Article 3

We have an absolute right to this article, but there are some important ways in which governments can interpret it.

Tasks

8 Elections are supposed to be held at reasonable intervals.
 a What might be the effect of too short an interval?
 b What might be the effect of too long an interval?
 c What do you think is a reasonable interval?
9 Why do you think it is important to guarantee a secret ballot?

Extension

Search newspapers and the Home Office website to find other examples of the impact of the Human Rights Act.

Miscarriages of justice

A **miscarriage of justice** occurs when a person is convicted and punished for a crime that they did not commit.

There are numerous reasons why miscarriages of justice occur, for example:
- non-disclosure of evidence by police or prosecution
- fabrication of evidence (that is, making it up)
- poor identification of individuals
- overestimation of the value of expert testimony
- unreliable confession (because of police pressure)
- because a defendant or perhaps a witness is psychologically unstable
- misdirection by a judge during trial.

Since the release of the high-profile Birmingham Six and Guildford Four – both of these groups were accused of terrorist offences – there have been many changes in the criminal justice system.

Development of the criminal justice system

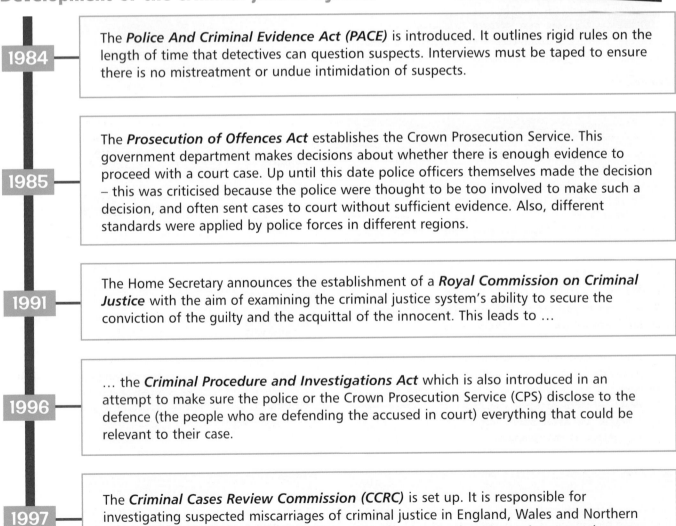

1984 — The *Police And Criminal Evidence Act (PACE)* is introduced. It outlines rigid rules on the length of time that detectives can question suspects. Interviews must be taped to ensure there is no mistreatment or undue intimidation of suspects.

1985 — The *Prosecution of Offences Act* establishes the Crown Prosecution Service. This government department makes decisions about whether there is enough evidence to proceed with a court case. Up until this date police officers themselves made the decision – this was criticised because the police were thought to be too involved to make such a decision, and often sent cases to court without sufficient evidence. Also, different standards were applied by police forces in different regions.

1991 — The Home Secretary announces the establishment of a *Royal Commission on Criminal Justice* with the aim of examining the criminal justice system's ability to secure the conviction of the guilty and the acquittal of the innocent. This leads to …

1996 — … the *Criminal Procedure and Investigations Act* which is also introduced in an attempt to make sure the police or the Crown Prosecution Service (CPS) disclose to the defence (the people who are defending the accused in court) everything that could be relevant to their case.

1997 — The *Criminal Cases Review Commission (CCRC)* is set up. It is responsible for investigating suspected miscarriages of criminal justice in England, Wales and Northern Ireland, and deciding whether or not to refer the case to the appropriate appeal court.

Since the 1980s an increasing number of organisations have been set up to campaign against miscarriages of justice and to lobby Parliament for changes to be made in the criminal justice system. Many campaigns are set up to publicise and gain support for individual cases of prisoners who say that they are innocent. There are also a growing number of support networks up and down the country made up of family, friends and supporters of wrongly convicted prisoners who have come together to help each other.

Case study

Stephen Downing was 17 years of age when he was sentenced to life imprisonment for the murder in 1973 of typist Wendy Sewell, in a cemetery where he worked. He signed a confession after being questioned by police for nine hours with no lawyer present. He had a reading age of just 11 and although he later withdrew his confession, it was still used as the basis for the prosecution case. At the original trial, a forensic examination of his bloodstained jeans had helped convict him, but an expert who looked again at the evidence expressed concerns over their value as evidence.

The conviction for murder was overturned in the Court of Appeal after Stephen had served 27 years in prison. Mr Downing was released from prison in February 2001 after he was granted bail by the appeal judges, who realised that an appeal was likely to succeed. The Court of Appeal declared the original conviction unsafe and ruled that neither the forensic evidence used at the trial nor the confession was conclusive.

COMMENT

> *Don Hale, the journalist and human rights campaigner who fought to secure Downing's release, spoke of the general feeling that Stephen Downing's case was exceptional: 'That is patently untrue: we've seen a stream of innocent men released from jail over the past few years but the Home Office still refuses to admit that the system gets it wrong.'*
>
> from Amelia Hill, 'Robert Brown won't get parole – because he maintains his innocence of murder', in *Guardian Unlimited*, 3 March 2002

> *Chris Mullin MP, a former journalist for TV's 'World In Action', said: 'Miscarriages of justice can occur under any system and I have no doubt they will occur in the future. We should never be complacent. The system has improved considerably since the big miscarriages of the mid-1970s. PACE, which came in 1984, has regulated interviews and improved the treatment of suspects, and just about all interrogations are now recorded. But the most important change is that people who believe they are the victims of miscarriages of justice have somewhere to go: the CCRC.'*
>
> adapted from:
> **www.bbc.co.uk – news section**

> *Paddy Hill, one of the Birmingham Six, said: 'Justice is something that is not on this government's curriculum.' He said the criminal justice system needed a radical overhaul to make it 'more open and accountable'. Mr Hill would like to see:*
> - *juries forced to give their verdicts in writing, to amplify on their reasons and guard against the danger of 'perverse' verdicts*
> - *judges and other judicial officials being elected, rather than chosen by 'the establishment'.*
>
> adapted from:
> **www.bbc.co.uk – news section**

Tasks

1 What changes have been introduced in the criminal justice system since Stephen Downing was convicted?

2 Do you think that Stephen Downing would have been convicted for the offence in today's courts?

3 List a set of arguments both for and against judges and other judicial officials being elected, rather than chosen by 'the establishment'.

4 What compensation do you think would be appropriate for Mr Downing?

Extension

Carry out some research into current campaigns about miscarriages of justice. Do you think enough has been done within the judicial system to ensure that miscarriages don't happen again in the future?

Stephen Downing could have been released on parole in 1990 if he had admitted killing Miss Sewell, but he always maintained his innocence. To date, Stephen Downing is Britain's longest-running miscarriage of justice.

Does Britain want to have a global influence?

During the 18th and 19th centuries Britain possessed a huge empire. Now the days of empire are long gone, but Britain still has connections with its former colonies through the Commonwealth (see the map on this page). Britain has also developed strong links with Europe, and a 'special relationship' with the USA. As a result, many people believe that Britain plays an important role on the international stage and that foreign policy and domestic policy are just as important as each other, as one affects the other.

Tony Blair's speech (Source A) sparked a debate in the media about Britain's role in world affairs. Sources B and C are both from *The Guardian*, a national newspaper.

SOURCE B

One in 20 of the people opening this *Guardian* (62,000 out of 1,204,000 on the latest readership figures) come directly, or indirectly, from India, Pakistan and Bangladesh. And the ethnic proportions are not so very different for the *Times* and *Independent*. Who can argue with Tony Blair when he says that 'foreign policy and domestic policy are part of the same thing'?

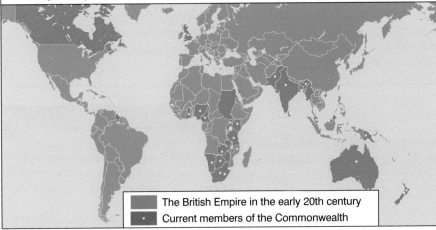

Some countries are excluded from the Commonwealth when they break the rules, for example Pakistan in 1999 and Zimbabwe in 2002.
They can rejoin when they meet the Commonwealth requirements.

The British Empire in the early 20th century
Current members of the Commonwealth

The British Empire and Commonwealth members today

Source A is an extract from Tony Blair's foreign policy speech in Bangalore, India in January 2002. It shows what the government at that time wanted Britain's role in world affairs to be.

SOURCE A

Britain can play a pivotal role in world affairs. The country has connections with many different regions ... Britain has the fourth largest economy in the world but our land mass and population constrain us. We are not a superpower, but we can act as a pivotal partner, working with others to make sense of this global interdependence, and make it a force for good for our own nation and the wider world... Our past gives us huge, unparalleled connections with many different regions of the world... The opportunity, therefore, is obvious. It shouldn't be exaggerated and I stress the role is as partner... The challenge, however, is to throw ourselves into this role with confidence, to discard isolationism, or retreat into nostalgia.

SOURCE C

Britain is undoubtedly one of the world's most powerful, rich and influential countries. The mistakes and misconceptions that cloud its days of empire, its vast diplomatic experiences, and present-day morality, imply a duty and responsibility to set an example and, occasionally, to lead.

adapted from
The Guardian, 7 January 2002

Is Britain important on the international stage?

The following pages look at Britain's relationships with the Commonwealth, the USA and Europe. The information and tasks on these pages will help you decide whether you agree or disagree with Tony Blair that 'Britain can play a pivotal role in world affairs'. After his speech in January 2002, there was criticism from some people. Sources D and E are examples of how the speech was criticised.

SOURCE D

The Tories accuse Blair of media grandstanding

Conservative leader Iain Duncan Smith has launched a fierce attack on Tony Blair's 'utopian' foreign policy, accusing the Prime Minister of 'media grandstanding'.

His comments follow Tony Blair's speech in India about Britain being a 'force for good' for both itself and the wider world. In his speech Mr Duncan Smith, who has criticised the Prime Minister for ignoring domestic issues because of the international agenda, called Mr Blair's foreign policy 'profoundly misguided'.

He said: 'The Prime Minister seems to believe that there are no limits to what Britain, acting as part of an all-embracing global coalition of the righteous, can and should do to make the world a better place. Trying to pursue ambitious foreign policy that outstrips a country's resources but does not advance its interests, puts a nation's safety and standing at risk,' Mr Duncan Smith argued.

adapted from: www.bbc.co.uk, 31 January 2002

SOURCE E

Tony Blair tours the world and the American empire expands

It is not evident that Mr Blair has really profited at home from his assertion of global leadership. The British press has treated it as confusion and spin by a Labour leadership in trouble because of the continued decline in British schools, health service and transport performance. Mr Blair arrived home from his latest trip to find new rail strikes and transport breakdowns.

In a conversation with reporters in Bangalore, India, Mr Blair brushed off former Secretary of State Dean Acheson's comment about postwar Britain having lost an empire without finding a role to replace it, saying it was not a valid comment.

adapted from: www.converge.org.nz, 14 January 2002

Tasks ?

Read source A.

1 Which 'regions' does Britain have connections with?
2 What does Tony Blair mean when he refers to 'Britain's past'?
3 What does **isolationism** mean?

Look at source B.

4 What point do you think the author is trying to make? Do you agree that 'foreign policy and domestic policy are part of the same thing'?

Look at source C.

6 How do you think people in other countries, especially former colonies of Britain, would feel about Britain taking a leadership role in the world?
7 Do you think Britain is in a position to 'to set an example and, occasionally, to lead' in global relations? Give reasons for your opinion.

As sources D and E show, not everyone agreed with Tony Blair's picture of what Britain's role in world affairs could be.

8 Make a list of all the points of criticism of Blair's speech. Which criticisms do you agree with?
9 What might happen if Britain did not try to get involved in the rest of the world?

Britain and Europe

The European Union today

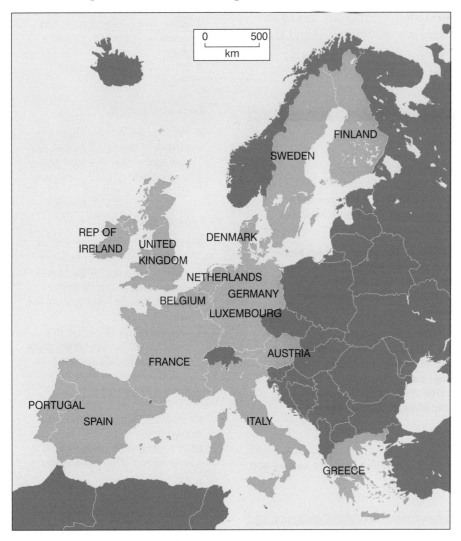

▲ **Countries in which the EU makes decisions**

The European Union is the framework for economic and political co-operation between European countries (15 states in 2002, with more preparing to join). The EU also oversees issues as wide-ranging as the environment, transport and employment, and has an increasing influence in foreign and defence policy.

It has five declared objectives:
- to promote economic and social progress
- to assert the identity of the European Union on the international scene
- to introduce European citizenship
- to develop an area of freedom, security and justice
- to maintain and build on established EU law.

Officially, the **European Union** has only existed since the early 1990s, although the term has been used for much longer than that. The Maastricht Treaty renamed what had been the European Community, the 'European Union', by creating what are known as the **three pillars** of the EU:
- European Community
- Common Foreign and Security Policy
- Justice and Home Affairs.

The first of these is managed by the institutions of the EU, while the second and third work through inter-governmental co-operation.

The *European Community* is responsible for the single market and freedom of movement across borders. It also looks after economic and monetary union, and issues such as agriculture, environment and competition. In order to achieve success in these areas, member states have given up some of their sovereignty, and EU institutions can act independently of the national governments. This means that individual countries sometimes end up following rules they would not have chosen for themselves.

In the second pillar, *Common Foreign and Security Policy*, member states aim to hold common positions and take joint action on foreign and security affairs. The aim for *Justice and Home Affairs* is to integrate member states' policies on asylum and immigration, customs, drugs and crime, through increased co-operation. The EU has enabled everyone to travel freely between member countries, and this has created a need for police to work more closely together, as criminals and smugglers find it easier to travel across borders too.

Britain out... then in...

Britain did not become a member of the European Union (which was called the European Community, EC or 'Common Market' at that time) until 1973. British politicians did not really start to think seriously about joining the EC until the 1960s. Up until then there seemed to be several powerful reasons to prevent Britain from joining (see the box below).

The absence of 'European feeling'
- Many British people and leaders objected to giving up some of the British government's power to a body outside the British Parliament.
- The British Empire was still in existence. This was something for Britain to be proud of – much more so, it appeared, than a European Union.

Economic reasons
Only 25% of Britain's trade was with Europe in the 1940s. Most of it was with the Empire, and later the Commonwealth, which produced food and raw materials for Britain. The Empire could not be brought into the EC along with Britain.

Defence reasons
Britain preferred not to be involved in Europe and relied heavily on what it called its 'special relationship' with America. It felt that the North Atlantic Treaty Organisation (NATO) alliance was enough – NATO ensured co-operation between Europe and the USA.

What happened to make Britain change its mind?

In 1959 Britain established the European Free Trade Association (EFTA), as a rival to the EU.

EFTA	European Community
Austria, Britain, Denmark, Norway, Portugal, Sweden, Switzerland	Belgium, France, Italy, Luxembourg, Netherlands, West Germany
Population without Britain: 38 million	Population without Britain: 200 million
Free trade area, no trade taxes	Free trade area developing
No other common policies	Other common policies included iron and steel, atomic energy, farming and fishing

Between 1958 and 1964, Europe became more attractive to British politicians:
- the total income of EU members increased by 68% and Britain's by 36%
- European industry increased in size by 49% and Britain's by 31%
- the average income of each person increased in Europe by 51% and in Britain by 23%
- Britain's trade with the Commonwealth increased by 1.6% and with the EU by 98%.

By the late 1960s Britain had lost most of its empire.

British entry

In 1961 the British Conservative government applied to join the EU. Five out of the six countries were delighted to accept Britain's late entry. However, General de Gaulle (President of France) said that Britain was too closely tied to America and was not really European enough to join the EU. Britain could do little about this. In 1967 the Labour government once again applied to join. This time General de Gaulle said the British were 'not quite ready'.

In 1971 Britain applied again. By this time de Gaulle was no longer the President of France, and the British application was accepted. In 1973 the Prime Minister, Edward Heath, signed Britain's acceptance of the Treaty of Rome.

Tasks

1 Why do you think Britain set up EFTA?
2 What statistics would you select as most helpful to make the case for Britain's entry to the EU by 1964?
3 Why do you think Britain eventually joined the EU?
4 Do you feel like an EU citizen? How is being an EU citizen different from being a British citizen?
5 Some people think the increased co-operation on defence policy may lead to a single EU army. What advantages and disadvantages can you think of for an EU army?
6 a Why do you think the EU is so heavily involved in issues such as fishing, farming, trade and the environment?
 b Can you think of any areas of government activity that the EU is *not* involved in?

Extension

Ask a group of young people about their attitude to Europe. Ask a group of older people the same questions. Compare their answers, and think about possible reasons for any differences.

The debate about Europe

Of course not everyone was 'happy' when Britain joined the EU back in 1971 (see source A). Not much has changed since then – there are still groups that would prefer Britain not to be a full member of the EU. In the 2001 general election the main topic of debate on Europe was whether Britain would be part the single currency, the Euro.

SOURCE A

We're in – but without the fireworks

Britain passed peacefully into Europe at midnight last night without any special celebration. Yesterday the latest opinion poll suggested that 38 per cent were happy about embarking on what Mr Heath depicted as an exciting adventure, while 39 per cent would prefer to get off. Twenty-three per cent had no opinion at all.

One of Britain's two Common Market Commissioners, said: 'This is a unique new year. What dictators have failed to do by force, democracies are undertaking by peaceful consent. Twenty-five years from now, if we build the right foundations in 1973, our children will enjoy a richer quality of life than had we remained separate. European civilisation will be able to speak in a united way that can contribute to a more peaceful and prosperous world.'

On the other side, the general secretary of the print worker's union was confident that the British people would long remember 1 January 1973 as 'the blackest day in the calendar of their history'. Wars and international conflict had at least left us with our basic national sovereignty and independence but that had now gone.

The Campaign for British Freedom said in a pamphlet that it was all a 'shameful betrayal'.

adapted from David McKie and Dennis Barker, 1 January 1973

SOURCE B

At the election, the Conservative Party will be fighting tooth and nail to keep the pound. We will be fighting to keep the pound because we believe it is in our national interest to maintain the flexibility to run our economy to suit British interests. And we will be fighting to keep the pound because above all we want to be able to assess how ultimately it will affect our ability as a nation to govern our own affairs.

from a speech by William Hague MP, former Conservative Party Leader, to party members in Huddersfield on 8 February 2001

SOURCE C

Blair: UK has no future outside Europe

The Prime Minister made the most explicitly pro-European speech of his premiership today, condemning Britain's old-fashioned view of the EU. The speech was both in praise of European co-operation and in sorrow for missed British opportunities spanning more than 50 years.

Mr Blair said: 'First we said it wouldn't happen, then we said it wouldn't work, then we said we wouldn't need it and Britain was left behind at every step of the way. The tragedy for British politics – for Britain – has been that politicians of both parties have consistently failed, not just in the 1950s but on up to the present day, to appreciate the emerging reality of European integration. And in doing so, they have failed Britain's interests.' He concluded: 'If this dismal history teaches us one clear lesson, it is this: the EU has succeeded and will succeed.' He said: 'The argument is simple. We are part of Europe. It affects us directly and deeply. Therefore we should exercise leadership in order to change Europe in the direction we want. Britain has no economic future outside Europe.'

adapted from Matthew Tempest in *The Guardian*, 23 November 2001

SOURCE D

▽ Why do some people want to save the pound?

EIGHT DAYS TO SAVE A POUNDING!

▲ **SOURCE E**

What does this cartoonist think was the reason behind the Conservatives' backing of the Save the Pound campaign?

Tasks

1 Compare source A, written in 1973, with those written in 2000/01 (sources B and C). Make a list of the similarities and differences between the articles.
   Has much changed?
2 Copy and complete the table (see right). Sources B, C and D will help you get started, but you should add your own ideas.
3 Why do you think the EU has always been such a divisive issue for British people and politicians?
4 Do you think Britain wants to be, or needs to be, an influential country within Europe?
   • If so, is being part of the 'Euro' zone the only way Britain can achieve this?
   • If not, what should Britain do?

   a State your own view.
   b Examine both sides of the argument.
   c Discuss the different views that have developed over time.
   d Explain your conclusion.

Being part of the EU, with the Euro:	
Advantages	**Disadvantages**

Britain and the Commonwealth

Fact Box

FOUNDED: 1931

MEMBERS: 54 states

POPULATION: 1.7 billion (30% world's population)

The Commonwealth used to be known as the 'British Commonwealth of Nations'. It is an association of former colonies, dependencies and other territories, plus Mozambique, which has no historical ties with Britain. It was after the independence of India and Pakistan in 1947 that the Commonwealth defined its modern shape. It dropped the word 'British' from its name, and no longer required members to swear allegiance to the Crown. However, the British monarch remains the official head of the Commonwealth. The heads of government of its member states hold Commonwealth heads of government meetings every two years to discuss issues of common interest.

Members commit themselves to the statement of beliefs set out by the heads of government (see source A). In 1995, a Commonwealth Ministers Action Group was set up to deal with governments that persistently break the Commonwealth principles. It can take such disciplinary measures as imposing sanctions or suspending members. For example, in 1995 it suspended Nigeria's membership after the military regime there passed the death sentence on the writer Ken Saro-Wiwa and a group of fellow activists. In 2000 it suspended Fiji following the overthrow of its elected government.

SOURCE A

The heads of government of the countries of the Commonwealth reaffirm their confidence in the Commonwealth as a voluntary association of sovereign independent states. We reaffirm our full and continuing commitment to these principles:

- International peace and order, global economic development and the rule of international law are essential to the security and prosperity of mankind.

- We believe in liberty and equality and in the individual's right to participate by means of free and democratic political processes in the society in which he or she lives.

- Economic and social development is vital to satisfy the basic needs and aspirations of the vast majority of the people of the world.

We pledge the Commonwealth and our countries to work with renewed energy, concentrating especially in the following areas:

- democracy, the rule of law and the independence of the judiciary, just and honest government

- human rights, including equal rights and opportunities for all citizens regardless of race, colour, creed or political belief

- equality for women, so that they may exercise their full and equal rights

- access to education

- the promotion of sustainable development and the relief of poverty

- the freest possible flow of trade on terms fair to all, taking account of the special requirements of developing countries

- an adequate flow of resources from the developed to developing countries, and action to help with the debt burdens of developing countries

- action to combat drug trafficking and abuse and communicable diseases

- support of the United Nations and other international institutions in the world's search for peace, disarmament and effective arms control.

adapted from the Harare Principles – Issued by Heads of Government in Harare, Zimbabwe, 20 October 1991

There are four criticisms in the statements below, and four positive statements. Sort out the statements into two groups and then try to match any cards that relate to the same issue.

1
To its members the Commonwealth is a voluntary association of independent states.

2
Some people argue that because action requires agreement, often not enough happens to punish dangerous states.

3
It does not act as a bloc in international affairs and so has little influence over non-members who may not act within its principles.

4
The countries in the Commonwealth are often so different that agreement can be difficult.

5
The Commonwealth has been called a post-colonial club – Britain's response to losing its empire.

6
The Commonwealth tries to promote democracy, good government, human rights and economic development.

7
Some believe that the encouragement of open discussion, occasionally leading to agreement, is a positive model to promote.

8
Members of the Commonwealth share a common heritage in many fields, especially in language.

The Commonwealth needs to be 'shaken up'

Commonwealth heads of government meet in Australia in March 2002

Suggested reforms:
- Appoint a president to speak on behalf of the Commonwealth on the world stage.
- Move the Commonwealth Secretariat (headquarters) out of London to somewhere like Cape Town or New Delhi, to show member nations that Britain's attitude has changed.
- Set out a new declaration of democracy and human rights, and appoint an 'enforcer' to investigate breaches of human rights and democracy.
- Create a permanent council of High Commissioners to act quickly in a crisis.

If the Commonwealth is to survive and recapture its early idealism then these reforms are urgent. The Commonwealth appears for a few days every two years when its heads of government meet, and then disappears. Unless it develops a permanent presence that allows it to respond to crises, it will never be effective. Re-inventing Britishness and re-inventing the Commonwealth are two sides of the same coin. Two-thirds of British youngsters have a cousin in another Commonwealth country. Forging a new and equal relationship with the Commonwealth will help us come to terms with our multicultural identity.

adapted from a report from The Foreign Policy Centre

Tasks

1 Why do you think the word 'British', and allegiance to the Crown, were dropped?
2 What other international organisations do you know about that pursue similar aims?

Class debate

Work as a class, in four groups. Two groups will argue *for* the motion; the other two groups will argue *against* it:
Motion: The Commonwealth is past its 'sell-by date'. It is time to look towards the future rather than to the past; it is time to dissolve the Commonwealth.

Extension

Having heard both sides of the argument, what do *you* think? Write down your own ideas about whether the Commonwealth should be reformed or dissolved. Use evidence where possible to support your opinion.

Britain and the USA

Is there really a 'special relationship' between Britain and the USA? The two countries have many things in common:

● Parts of the USA were once ruled as a colony by Britain, until the USA gained independence in 1776 following a war with Britain.
● Britain and the USA share a language and many elements of their cultures.
● They were close allies during the First and Second World Wars, and the Cold War.
● After the Second World War, the USA made large loans available to help Britain's recovery.
● British and American governments have often co-operated in defence issues, and international affairs.

Tasks ?

1 Copy and complete the 'brainstorm' diagram with as many links as you can think of:

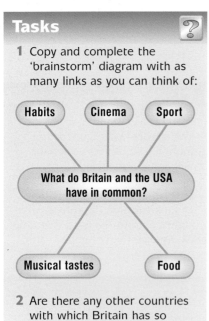

Habits **Cinema** **Sport**

What do Britain and the USA have in common?

Musical tastes **Food**

2 Are there any other countries with which Britain has so much in common?
3 Does having so much in common make it inevitable that the two countries are going to get on well with each other – have 'a special relationship'?

Focus on the War Against Terrorism

> We, here in Britain, stand shoulder to shoulder with our American friends in this hour of tragedy and we, like them, will not rest until this evil is driven from our world.

Tony Blair, British Prime Minister, 11 September 2001

WANTED
DEAD OR ALIVE
Osama bin Laden
For mass murder in New York City

▲ Osama bin Laden, the leader of al-Qaida, was believed to be responsible for the attacks

▲ 11 September 2001: the Twin Towers of the World Trade Center in New York were destroyed by terrorists, killing more than 3,000 people

The response to this attack was the American President's declaration of a 'War Against Terrorism'. The American government was trying to create a global coalition, and George Bush famously stated: 'You are either with us or with the terrorists'. In reality, as Sir Michael Boyce, the British Chief of Defence Staff, put it: 'the US – the world's only superpower with the capability of launching military strikes anywhere in the world – has less need of consensus than we do.' Despite this, Britain emerged as one of the strongest supporters of the campaign. Was this another example of the 'special relationship' at work?

Does the USA value its 'special relationship' with Britain? Does Britain really need a special relationship with the USA? Look at the following sources and make up your own mind.

SOURCE A ▷

▽ SOURCE B

A tale of two conflicts
AMERICA AND BRITAIN FIGHT DIFFERENT WARS

It is in the nature of coalitions that they play down their differences in favour of the things that unite them. In the case of the international coalition against terrorism, these unifying goals seem big and familiar: to hunt down and bring to justice the perpetrators of the September 11 attacks, and to work by many means to prevent repeat attacks.

Yet, while there is general agreement about them, there is also disagreement on other goals, including where the campaign goes from here.

In the US report, the response to the attacks on New York and Washington is American-led, American-defined and American-executed. No-one else rates a mention. George Bush is portrayed as an all-wise law enforcer, military leader, coalition builder and deliverer of humanitarian aid who is 'implementing a comprehensive and visionary foreign policy'. Anyone who imagines that Britain and Tony Blair loom large in the American mind is in for a disappointment. Neither of them receives a mention in the White House account.

The British version describes a campaign in which America is merely one player among a vast array, and at times is almost marginal.

These documents are propaganda for different domestic audiences. But the stories they tell are so different that it is hard not to sense that either the Americans or the British – or both – are seriously deceiving themselves about the extent of their common purpose.

adapted from *The Guardian*, 22 December 2001

▽ SOURCE C

Blair Visit Strengthens the 'Special Relationship'

The 'special relationship' between Britain and America has tended to be a much overworked expression. Both countries have employed it when it was useful, but ignored it when they wanted.

But in New York and Washington this week it became real. Tony Blair recalled the spirit of the Blitz when, he said, America stood by Britain. President Bush said that the United States truly had no better friend in the world than Britain.

adapted from George Jones in *The Daily Telegraph*, 22 September 2001

Tasks

4 What message does the cartoonist present about the 'special relationship' in source A?
5 What are the two conflicts described in source B?
6 Does the author of source B believe there is a special relationship?
7 Why do you think politicians sometimes 'use' the idea of the special relationship, as suggested in source C?
8 Using all the sources and other information you may have about the 'War Against Terrorism', list the arguments for and against the special relationship in this case.

The United Nations

Britain and the United Nations

Britain has been a member of the United Nations (UN) since it was established at the end of the Second World War. All member states meet together in the UN Assembly, but Britain has been more influential than most countries because it has always been a member of the Security Council. The UN cannot employ troops unless the Security Council agrees unanimously, and this gives a relatively small number of countries a great deal of power. The Security Council is made up of Britain, France, Russia, China and the USA, plus ten other nations elected from the Assembly for two-year terms each. The five permanent members have a veto on any decision and so they hold significant power in the UN.

What is the UN for?

The UN has three basic aims:
1 To maintain peace.
2 To encourage friendly relations between countries.
3 To help countries develop economically and socially.

What does the UN do?

Whilst the UN is based on just three simple aims, it has grown to be a huge organisation, which comprises a network of organisations, each specialising in its own area.

Peacekeepers

You may have seen UN peacekeepers employed in conflict situations all over the world – UN soldiers are easy to spot because of their blue helmets, and their tanks and vehicles are painted white. Because the UN has so many member states (almost every country in the world), it is possible for it to co-ordinate troops from places that are unaffected by conflicts. This means that the soldiers, and the countries they come from, are unlikely to be too committed to one side of the conflict or another, and are therefore able to separate sides in a conflict, and help to maintain peace.

It has also been possible for particular countries, such as the USA and Britain, to put forward a resolution to the UN Security Council which gives them permission to undertake action against a country on behalf of the UN. For example, the USA and some EU countries, including Britain, took a leading role in driving the Iraqi army out of Kuwait in 1991, and US planes and personnel stayed on after the action to police a 'no-fly zone' in Iraqi air space.

United Nations Children's Emergency Fund (UNICEF)

UNICEF is the only UN organisation that does not receive funding from the UN. It raises money directly from governments and by fund-raising activities. It works in over 160 countries to help meet children's rights to health, food, education, water and sanitation. It works in partnership with local charities and governments to provide services to meet the needs of children and promote their rights.

In the UK, UNICEF promotes children's rights, works with others who are helping children, and raises money to support its international work. In 2000, it raised over £21 million for UNICEF programmes.

United Nations High Commissioner for Refugees (UNHCR)

The UNHCR focuses its efforts on the 22 million people around the world who are uprooted from their homes. It aims to support the human rights of refugees, and to make sure they are not returned to countries where they face persecution.

It runs refugee camps when emergencies happen and where emergency relief is needed. It also works with governments to help refugees settle in their new countries, and helps them later to return to their original homes if they want to when the situation improves.

United Nations Conference on Trade and Development (UNCTAD)

UNCTAD is the main part of the UN that deals with trade. It talks to countries to try to co-ordinate programmes to get them involved more (and fairly) with the international economy. It focuses specifically on the poorest countries and collects information to make sure that other decision-makers have accurate facts on which to make their own decisions. It has an annual budget of approximately £50 million a year.

It has organised international agreements about coffee, cocoa, sugar and timber trading. It has also produced guidelines to help manage debt.

United Nations Development Programme (UNDP)

The UNDP provides services directly to governments and to other UN agencies. This helps them develop policies and services in the following areas:

- democracy
- poverty reduction
- environmental issues and sustainable development
- gender
- HIV/AIDS
- crisis prevention and recovery.

Tasks

1 What do you think the UN gains from Britain's membership?
2 What does Britain gain from membership of the UN?
3 Britain gives financial support for the UN to provide all the services listed here. What else does Britain do to help in each of these areas of activity?
4 What other organisations do you know about that would help with each of the areas covered by UN agencies?

Extension

Choose *one* UN agency and carry out some further research. Find out what it does, why it does it, and examples of where it has failed and succeeded. You may choose another agency – there are links to many more at:
www.un.org
How effective do you think the UN is in achieving its aims?

Revision

Now that you have worked through Section 3, you should be able to answer the following short-answer questions. Once you have worked through the questions, check your answers with others in the class and with your teacher, and use the facts to start a set of revision cards. These can be completed as you work through other topic areas in your Citizenship Studies course.

A Short answers

1 What are the two Houses of Parliament?

2 How is the Prime Minister chosen?

3 Who chooses the members of the Cabinet?

4 Who carries out decisions made by government?

5 State **one** power held by the monarch.

6 State **one** power only held by the Prime Minister.

7 Which government department collects taxes?

8 Which government department spends the most?

9 What is **lobbying**?

10 What is **devolution**?

11 List two changes that were introduced by the Local Government Act 2000.

12 What is meant by the following terms:

   a criminal law?

   b civil law?

13 State **two** differences between a Magistrates' Court and a Crown Court.

14 List **three** different types of sentence a court can pass on an adult offender.

15 List **three** different types of sentence a court can pass on a young offender.

16 What is the EU?

17 What is the Commonwealth?

18 What is the UN?

19 List **three** ways in which Britain is influenced by the EU.

20 List **three** ways in which Britain contributes to the UN.

B   Source-based questions

'I would not give half a guinea* to live under one form of government rather than another. It is of no moment to the happiness of an individual.'

Samuel Johnson

* A guinea was an old coin.

1   In what ways does government have an impact on people's lives?

2   Do you agree that government has no impact on the happiness of an individual?

3   What do you think Samuel Johnson meant?

C   Extended answers

Write an essay on **one** of the following topics. Remember to use evidence, and consider the issue from different viewpoints. You may express your own opinion in the conclusion.

1   The Human Rights Act is important for UK citizens. Why?

- What does the Act say?
- What kinds of cases does it apply to?
- What does it mean for citizens?

2   'Britain has lost an empire and is still looking for a role in the world.' Do you agree?

- How has Britain played an important role in the world?
- What international organisations does Britain work with?
- Does Britain have a global role?

3   How does the criminal justice system shape the law? Describe:

- the role of the police
- the role of the courts
- specific examples of laws evolving.

D   Active ideas

You may choose to become involved in active experience relating to government and the law. The following are some ideas.

1   Plan an educational workshop or activity for other students to learn about the UN.

2   Conduct a survey on local issues about crime and policing, and report your findings to the local police.

3   Set up your own crime reduction group in school to cut down on specific issues affecting your school or local area.

4   Write to MPs and others who may be able to help on any issue that affects you and your local community.

5   Join a campaign organised by a voluntary organisation to put pressure on politicians to bring about change.

What it means to vote

To be effective citizens we need to be able to influence things, so that we can either maintain the things we agree on, or change those we disagree with. This section looks at the ways in which citizens can bring about change: by voting, by campaigning, by changing their lifestyle.

Voting is central to democracy. Governments generally try to act in ways that fulfil the promises they made at the last election, and persuade people to vote for them at the next election. In the UK each individual should count equally because we have a system of 'one person, one vote'. It was not always this way. In the past, some people had more votes if they were rich while others did not have a vote at all – for example, if they were female, or black, or did not own property. Such people, all over the world, have often had a long, difficult struggle to get the vote so that they can have control over what the government does.

Suffragettes

Before the 20th century, most men believed that women were incapable of making rational decisions about public life. Emily Davidson (see the photograph) was a member of the suffragette movement which fought for the right of women to vote. Over the course of more than 50 years of struggle for the vote, many other women held imaginative campaigns, protested, went to prison and went on hunger strikes.

▼ **In 1913, Emily Davidson died when she threw herself under the King's horse to draw attention to how strongly she felt about women's right to vote.**

The **franchise** (the people who can vote) has been extended over time:

1900 – Some men and all women were still unable to vote.

1918 – All men over 21 and most women over 30 received the vote.

1928 – The voting age for women was lowered to 21.

1969 – The voting age for men and women was lowered to 18.

Today only the following people cannot vote:
- those under 18 years of age
- members of the House of Lords
- those convicted within the previous five years of illegal or corrupt election practices
- foreign nationals, apart from citizens of Commonwealth countries and the Republic of Ireland who live in Britain
- patients who are detained in mental institutions because of criminal behaviour
- sentenced prisoners.

The electoral register

The electoral register is a list of all the names of people who are allowed to vote and who have registered their name with the authorities. Voting cards are sent out only to those people on the register. Your details are not automatically added to the register, so if you move home you must re-register at your new address. Homeless people are supposed to be able to vote but, in practice, they often cannot register as they do not have a fixed address.

Representation

In modern times, people do not have the time or the inclination to be fully involved in every policy decision. We elect representatives. The idea is that the Member of Parliament (MP) for a constituency should represent the interests of *all* his or her constituents (people in the constituency), even those who voted for other candidates.

But how representative are our representatives?

If an alien from outer space were to crash into the House of Commons, they would find a bizarre cross-section of Britons. Confronted by just 120 women and 10 Asians or black people out of a total of 659 MPs, our space traveller could be forgiven for thinking that this strange political race consisted of white men over 40. Stranger still, they would almost all be former teachers, lawyers and councillors. Typical of modern Britain they ain't.

from Paul Waugh *The Rough Guide to the Election 2001*

Parties

When people vote they select an individual candidate, but they may do so mainly because of the political party the candidate represents. Each political party writes a **manifesto** before the election, to say what they would do if they were elected as the government. Voters normally vote for the party whose manifesto most closely matches their own views on what is important. Voters may not act in this way if they dislike the candidate standing for that party in their constituency, or particularly like the candidate for another party. In the past people were often loyal to one party throughout their lives. Now many people change their allegiance (support) when they vote at different elections.

Free and fair

A **free election** is one in which nobody is forced in any way to vote for a particular individual or party – in other words, they are free to vote for whoever they choose. There have been allegations of violence and intimidation in a number of elections around the world. This means that the result does not reflect the will of the people. One of the important ways of ensuring that an election is free is to have a **secret ballot**. Nobody should be able to see where on the ballot paper you have marked the cross. When your ballot paper is put into the ballot box it is totally anonymous.

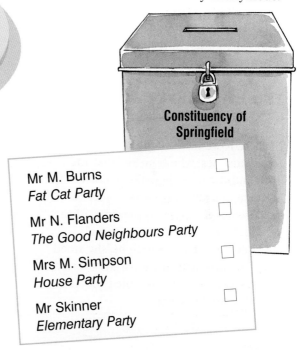

Constituency of Springfield

Mr M. Burns
Fat Cat Party

Mr N. Flanders
The Good Neighbours Party

Mrs M. Simpson
House Party

Mr Skinner
Elementary Party

Tasks

1 Look back at the list of people who are not allowed to vote. Do you think it is reasonable that these people are denied the vote?
2 Should people be able to vote when they are younger than 18? Or should they have to wait until they are older than 18?
3 a If you have a school council, what problems does your class representative have with representing the whole class?
  b What problems do you think an MP might have in representing the views of everyone in their constituency?
4 Why is voting considered so important?
5 How differently do you think governments would behave if there were no elections?

Extension

In groups, write a manifesto for a new political party.
a Look at existing manifestos: what are the main differences between parties?
b Write your manifesto: remember that any money spent by the elected government must be found from taxes or other sources.
c Do you think many people would vote for your party, or would it only be popular for people who are similar to yourselves?
d Share manifestos with others in the class and discuss the strengths and weaknesses of each.

Voting systems

The way in which votes are counted affects who governs us. There are many different systems for counting votes. The result of the 2001 UK election meant that the Labour Party formed the government after getting 40.7% of the national vote. The candidate representing Kidderminster Hospital (see page 101) took one seat in Parliament with 0.1% of the national vote, whilst the Greens got no seats with 0.6% of the vote.

This shows it is better for a small party to get all its votes in one constituency, rather than a few spread out in many constituencies.

The 'first past the post' system

In the UK we have single member constituencies, which means that the one candidate who gets the majority of the vote in each constituency goes to Parliament. He or she represents all the people in that constituency, and also represents the party which he/she stood for. The party with the most MPs forms the government. This is called the '**first past the post' system**.

▲ The candidates who come second and third in each constituency don't get a consolation prize

This system means that the party with the most votes throughout the country may not get the most seats. If Party X gets a lot of votes in *all* constituencies, spread quite evenly throughout the country, they may not win many seats in Parliament. Party Y may get fewer votes in total but have them all concentrated in half the constituencies – they would then win all those constituencies. The total number of votes throughout the country is not proportional to the total number of seats. The Liberal Democrats have suffered from this problem, as they gained 18% of the vote in 2001 but fewer than 8% of the seats in Parliament.

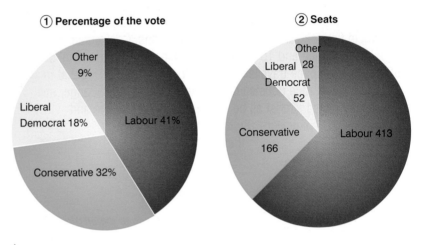

▲ **UK Election 2001**

For full information about the percentages of the vote and number of seats gained by each party, go to: **www.bbc.co.uk/vote2001** and click on Full UK Scoreboard.

Equal votes?

Central to democracy is the idea of 'one person, one vote', but critics of the current system argue that one vote is worth more in a marginal seat, where the first and second parties have a similar number of votes so the result cannot be predicted easily. In a 'safe seat', where the same party almost always wins, a voter may feel that their vote does not count at all. In the 2001 election, turnout was higher in marginal constituencies, where people felt their vote could make a difference, than in safe constituencies.

Tactical voting

With the 'first past the post' system, you may feel that voting for a party that normally gets about 3% of the vote in your constituency, is a wasted vote. You may decide to vote for your second choice, because at least they have a chance of winning. This is called **tactical voting**, and is increasingly common. There are Conservative-held seats where it would make sense for Liberal Democrats to vote Labour in order to unseat their MP. There are other Conservative-held seats where it would make sense for Labour voters to switch to the Liberal Democrats to unseat their MP. This means that the results in percentage of votes (see the pie chart) do not represent how people might have voted under a different system.

Alternatives to 'first past the post'

The alternative vote (AV) system

Voters rank-order the candidates on the ballot paper in single-member constituencies. If no candidate has over 50% on first preferences, the candidate with the lowest number of votes is eliminated and their votes are re-allocated. This is repeated with second preferences and then third until one candidate has over 50%.

The single transferable vote (STV) system

This system would be for larger constituencies with several representatives. Voters rank-order the candidates on the ballot paper. There can be more than one candidate for each party on the list. All the candidates receiving over a specified proportion of the vote are elected.

The additional member system (AMS)

Voters cast two votes: one for a constituency MP and one for a party list. This system is used for the London Assembly. It helps parties like the Greens get representatives elected. Although they did not win in any area, their level of support across London enabled them to have representatives selected from the party list.

> For a summary of different types of voting system, search for Independent Commission on the Voting System Glossary on: **www.archive.official-documents.co.uk**

'First past the post'

Advantages	Disadvantages
• One party forms the government, so the government is stable, strong and able to make policy without endless disagreements.	• Small parties get little say in Parliament.
• There is an MP for each constituency who represents the people of that constituency.	• The proportion of MPs for any party does not reflect the proportion of votes for that party.
• If the government does not keep the promises they made before the election, the people can vote them out at the next election (this would be harder with a coalition government).	• People who did not vote for the winning candidate in their constituency feel they are not represented.
• Counting ballot papers is easy.	• People's second choice is not taken into account.

Tasks

1 What factors influence how people vote?
2 Is your vote wasted if you vote for a party that only gets a small number of votes? Think of arguments for and against.
3 Can you add any advantages and disadvantages to the 'first past the post' table?
  Make tables of advantages and disadvantages for the other systems mentioned.
4 What voting system do you think would be the fairest?

Extension

If you did the extension activity on page 95, present your manifestos and hold elections under different electoral systems. Does the system affect the way you vote? Does it affect the result?
In the UK there are currently a number of different voting systems being used for different elections. Find out more about what election system is used for electing members of:
– the European Parliament (MEPs)
– the Scottish Parliament
– the Welsh Assembly
– the Greater London Assembly
– your local council.

Turnout

From 1955 to 1992, turnout at national UK elections averaged 75.8%. Turnout in the 2001 national election was only 59.4% of registered voters. Only 40% of young people (18–24-year-olds) voted. Turnout is even lower in European and local elections: the turnout in the 1999 European election was only 24%.

Low turnout is a problem for democracy:
- If most people do not vote, then it becomes more difficult for the government to be seen as representative or legitimate.
- It is a problem for the electorate, as they are not using their potential power to influence government.

Various reasons are given for low turnout.

> Sleaze leads to disillusionment with the whole political process.

> Everyone is happy with the state of the country.

> It's obvious who will win anyway.

> In 2001 a Gallup poll found that only 29% of voters believe there are really important differences between parties.

> No time to go to the polling station.

> Bad weather on polling day.

> Big business has more power than individual governments, so there's no point.

> What politicians go on about has nothing to do with me and my life.

A	Glossier campaign leaflets
B	A proportional representation voting system
C	A voting system where you made a list of preferences
D	A really bad government
E	Voting on the internet
F	Voting by telephone
G	More local government and less national government
H	More national government and less local government
I	More advertising by the political parties
J	More education about politics in schools
K	More honest politicians
L	Less jargon in campaigning
M	Having more female and black candidates
N	More information about how to contact your MP
O	Campaign leaflets aimed at specific groups (different ages, languages and interest groups)
P	A faster process for registering for the electoral roll
Q	Elections at weekends
R	Elections declared a public holiday
S	More local meetings where people can discuss issues with key political figures

Various ideas have been suggested to improve turnout. Some aim to address the disillusionment of voters, but many look at the actual voting process. Look at the suggestions A–S and decide which you think would be effective in increasing turnout.

Maybe apathy is not the cause of low turnouts. 'Mori found that political apathy was an issue for only 10% of young people, while the majority claimed they were interested in politics.'

'Politicians turn to Pop Idol for voter inspiration',
The Guardian,
11 February 2002

In Australia, voting is compulsory: people who are registered but who do not vote are fined. Obviously, you can put a blank or spoiled ballot paper in the box if you don't want to choose one of the candidates listed. A blank ballot paper is more meaningful than a low turnout, as politicians can see how many people are disillusioned with the system instead of speculating about why people did not turn out to vote. Some people feel that the compulsory system is wrong and that people should have a right not to vote.

Tasks

1 Why do you think turnout for young people is lower than average?
2 Why do you think turnout is lower in local and European elections than in general elections?
3 Will you vote when you are 18? Why/Why not?
4 Does low turnout mean that the government is less legitimate?
5 Go through the suggestions for improving turnout and explain how each one may help, or why it won't.

Discussion

Hold a classroom debate about the motion:
Should voting be compulsory in Britain?

Or have a classroom discussion about the following question:
In February 2002, 9 million votes were cast for the final of 'Pop Idol'. Other TV shows such as 'Big Brother' also attract huge numbers of votes. What could we learn from these shows to encourage votes for government elections?

Getting your voice heard

By conducting carefully planned campaigns to change the views of politicians, of important decision-makers and the public, charities and voluntary organisations have often been at the forefront of social change. In today's complex world, a range of campaigning skills are needed more than ever.

Organisations must use a variety of different techniques to ensure that their voice is heard at the highest level. Whether groups or individuals try to secure change at a local, national or international level, any successful campaign must have clear aims, both in terms of outcomes and of who to target.

So how do you run a successful campaign?

In the past there have been two main models of campaigning.

1 The 'inside track' means that groups have tried to use their influence, reputation and contacts to convince politicians and decision-makers of the merits of their cause.

▲ Sometimes it's not what you know but who you know that counts

2 The second approach has been more confrontational, using the media to expose issues in public and pressurising decision-makers by using the weight of public opinion.

Today campaigners need to be more sophisticated. They operate in a more competitive environment. If a group or an individual wants to be heard they often develop alliances and partnerships with other groups, and show that there is deep-rooted and widespread concern for their campaign. Local support networks are important because they show that the campaign connects with real people.

You can still get your voice heard, even without an 'inside track' to the top ▷

Tasks ?

1 a Look at the following list of campaigns and decide which are:
  – local
  – national
  – international.
 b Do any of them need to address more than one level of activity?
 • Debt relief for poor countries
 • Ban on fox-hunting
 • Improve road crossing near a school
 • Limit carbon emissions (global warming)
 • Speeding in cars
 • Nursery school closure
 • Licensing hours (pub opening and closing times)
 • Anti-'globalisation'

2 Look at the two approaches to campaigning outlined on this page. What are the advantages and disadvantages of each?

Extension

Get into groups and choose a particular charity or campaign. It could be a local, national or international issue. Create a display about the campaign, showing the following information:
– the aims of the campaign
– methods used by the campaigners to highlight their aims.

• Are their methods successful?
• How could you contribute to the campaign?

You may need to carry out some more research and collect examples of campaign material to complete your display.

Once the display is ready, spend some time going round the class, looking at other groups' work. Make a list of the variety of techniques used in these campaigns. Do any seem better than others?

Focus on Dr Richard Taylor – an independent Member of Parliament (MP)

In the 2001 general election, retired hospital consultant Dr Richard Taylor became the only independent MP. After having polled 58% of the vote in Wyre Forest he said, 'I am absolutely delighted the people have shown the government and the major political parties that they cannot be disregarded – that democracy does count'.

Candidate	1997	2001
Labour	26,843	10,857
Conservative	19,897	9,350
Independent	–	28,487

 Wyre Forest Election Results

What was his campaign about?

The campaign was based on the issue of saving and then restoring services to Kidderminster Hospital, re-opening the Accident and Emergency (A&E) department and in-patient services. Dr Taylor worked at the hospital for 23 years. In the early 1990s he raised over £400,000 for the cancer centre at the hospital and in 1997 he became chairman of the campaign to save services there.

The A&E department is now based at a new hospital in Worcester, 15 miles away. The plans also mean that there would no longer be any 'acute' beds for in-patients and the Kidderminster Hospital would be reduced to a walk-in centre for out-patients – anything serious would have to go to Worcester or elsewhere. The Kidderminster campaign argues that the surrounding area has too many people not to have its own casualty department. The government argues that the hospital is too small to be worth the money.

The issue of hospital or casualty closure is a powerful way of engaging the voter – as Dr Taylor put it: 'They have used the ballot box – the only weapon left to people who have been disregarded'. As the only independent, who defeated a former Labour minister, Dr Taylor is unlikely to have much power at Westminster, but his election sends out a very strong message to health authority bosses and leaders of government. Talking about his victory, Dr Taylor said: 'The message to the government is that you cannot ride roughshod over local community feelings without rebellion.'

Tasks ?

3 Why do you think Dr Taylor decided not to join a political party?

4 Why do you think he was elected to Parliament?

5 Do you think people are more concerned and therefore more likely to vote about local rather than national or international issues? Explain your answer.

6 Can you think of any local issues that people in your area would feel so strongly about?

7 Are there any drawbacks to having an independent MP, rather than a member of a party?

8 How effective is standing for election as a way to get things changed?

101

Campaigning and the media

The media has a very useful role to play in campaigning. All groups who are trying to raise awareness of their issues use some form of media to highlight their cause and to get the public's attention and support.

Look at the campaigning material on these pages and collect some examples of other campaigns. How successful are they in getting their message across?

Tasks [?]

1 Copy out and complete this assessment chart:

Message clear and to the point?	/5
Balance between words and images?	/5
Strong impact	/5
Likely to make people interested?	/5
TOTAL	/20

2 **Comment**
  a What do you like the most about the campaigning material?
  b What do you like the least about the campaigning material?
3 Do you think any of the materials are likely to have an impact on people who are not already interested in that issue? Explain your answer.
4 Take the least successful example you have looked at. What would you do to improve it?
5 Do you think it is justifiable to use any image in a good cause?

The cost of your week's coffee could help provide Zoe's village with clean water.

It's amazing how much money you can spend without thinking about it. When, just 50p a day could help provide children in desperate need with access to clean water, health services and education. As a registered charity, EveryChild is involved in 84 projects in 18 countries worldwide. With over 20 years experience of fighting poverty, we ensure that over £12 in every £15 sponsorship donation goes to support our work overseas. So why not have something to show for your money?

50p a day can make a difference call **020 8000**

Yes, I would like to give a child a better chance in life.
☐ I wish to sponsor a child. I enclose my first monthly payment of £15. (Cheques payable to EveryChild)
☐ Please send me more information about Child Sponsorship
☐ I will pay by ☐ MasterCard ☐ Visa ☐ Switch/Issue No☐

Expiry date: ☐☐ - ☐☐

Postcode

Email

Please complete this coupon and return it to EveryChild, FREEPOST LON21175, London EC2B 2BA

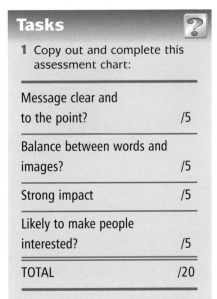

MATERIAL WORLD: 80% OF THE RUBBISH PRODUCED WEEKLY BY AN AVERAGE HOUSEHOLD COULD BE RECYCLED

Every child deserves to do more than just survive

For many children living in the developing world, every day is a struggle to survive. They often wake up hungry, work in their parents' fields for long hours just to help their families scrape by. It is no wonder there is little opportunity for them to realise their potential.

These children live in abject poverty which affects their entire lives. In Africa, Latin America and large areas of Asia poverty deprives children of growing up healthy and having an education. If they learned to read and write, they would have so many more opportunities in the future.

We don't believe this is any life for children. Every child deserves clean water, nourishing food, good health and a basic education.

If you agree, please become a Plan child sponsor today. Child sponsorship gives communities and their children the chances they so desperately need to live the lives they deserve.

Give children the life they should have

We know that children can only realise their potential by living in a thriving family and community that has skills and resources which bring self-sufficiency and dignity to everyone.

As well as providing the funds which enable projects to happen, many sponsors have a more personal relationship through the exchange of letters and photos with their sponsored child. Sponsored children look forward to receiving messages of support which boost their self-esteem. In return, sponsors hear about what's going on in the community and get a unique insight into a different culture.

Every project Plan commits to provides practical, long-term support for the whole community. For example, latrines and a clean water supply help children grow up healthy. A school gives children the chance to learn skills for the future which they can pass on to the next generation. A health centre means more children will be vaccinated against diseases.

Plan's goal is to be able to reach the point when a community doesn't need us anymore and we can move on to another community in need of our help.

Through child sponsorship we are helping ten million people in the developing world to make lasting changes to their lives.

"I need to drink clean water"

"There is only dirty water in our village. Just one drink can give me and my friends bad stomachs and make us very sick."

Every minute 10 people die from drinking dirty water in the developing world.

Last year Plan provided materials and training so villagers could build 20,493 water wells and helped communities to have clean, safe water. We couldn't have done it without our sponsors.

"I should be able to go to school"

"My parents can't afford to send me to school. But if I learnt to read and write then I could get a proper job when I grow up."

More than 130 million school age children in the developing world have no access to basic education.

Last year Plan helped villagers to build or improve 2,680 classrooms, we trained 20,638 teachers and distributed 287,541 school books. We couldn't have done it without our sponsors.

"I want to grow up healthy"

"If I get ill my mother and I have to walk for hours to the hospital in the nearest town nine miles away."

In some developing countries, Niger, for example, the mortality rate for children under five is over 40 times higher than in the UK.

Last year Plan provided training for villagers to build over 18,348 much-needed health clinics and trained 48,008 community health workers. We couldn't have done it without our sponsors.

I want more than this

Discover how child sponsorship can give children the life they should have

Plan
Be a part of it.

Campaigning and the internet

The internet allows campaigns to be organised across national boundaries. People all over the world can access information from the internet, so long as they have the right equipment. If you look at the websites of a whole range of campaigning organisations you will see that there is no agreement about what constitutes 'net activism'. Getting involved with organisations via their websites means different things on each site. Some organisations want you to donate funds, others want you to download information on how to lobby politicians or important decision-makers, while others seek individual participation through specific acts like signing a petition or sending a virtual postcard.

Fact Box

At the end of the 1990s:

- 32% of UK households were connected to the internet

- 45% of British adults – equivalent to more than 20 million people – had access to the internet at some time.

Tasks

Look at the sample web page opposite.

1 List the number of ways the web page encourages you to get involved with the organisation and its campaigns.
2 What do you think are the advantages and disadvantages of encouraging individual participation using the internet?

The Internet has the potential to make us all global campaigners.

Extension

Survey: Do people visit the websites of campaigning organisations?

Devise a survey to find out if people visit and/or participate in campaigning websites.

You can use the following structure, or look back at Section 1 'Skills' to remind you about how to structure a survey and create your own. Try to survey a minimum of ten people.

1 Have you ever visited a campaigning organisation's website?   yes / no
Which ones? (list):

2 If no, why not?

3 If yes, why did you visit the site?
  a General information about the organisation ☐
  b Specific information about an issue or campaign ☐
  c By chance ☐
  d Someone recommended it ☐

4 Did you actively get involved with the organisation?   yes / no

5 If no, why not?

6 If yes, how?
  a By registering my e-mail details to be kept in regular contact ☐
  b Downloaded campaigning information ☐
  c Sent a virtual postcard ☐
  d Signed a petition ☐
  e E-mailed the site to a friend ☐
  f Other (please explain) ☐

Conclusion

Thinking about getting involved in campaigns, which of the following statements would you agree with:
a The internet is largely irrelevant to people.
b The internet could encourage people to get involved but it does not seem to have made much of a difference yet.
c The internet encourages many more people to get involved in campaigns.

www.lunchbreak.co.uk

Welcome to Lunch Break

The Official Home of the Campaign for Longer Lunches

Run by students for the good of students, we are campaigning to stop the shortening of lunch breaks across the country.

Click on links to find out more about who we are, why we exist, what we want and how to get involved.

We need your money to start a nationwide poster campaign. We will send posters to every school to put up in their canteens, staff rooms and lobbies.

CLICK   Click here to donate money

We need to gather evidence that you, the students, want longer lunch breaks. Tell us your views and share your ideas with us.

CLICK   Click here to participate in our survey

We want to build up a network of student groups in schools across the country. This section will tell you how to get a registration pack and information about how to start.

CLICK   Click here to find out about starting up your own group

This automatic e-mail will take your message direct to the Department for Education and Skills. Tell the Minister what you want and why you want it. The bigger the response, the more chance they will sit up and listen.

CLICK   Click here to send a message to the government

This section contains our backdated newsletters, facts and figures from small-scale surveys we have carried out, and information about the management committee.

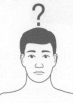

CLICK   Click here for more information

Find out what other school groups have been doing – what has worked and what has failed. Pick up some ideas for how to manage your own campaign.

CLICK   Click here for case studies

Individual changemakers (1)

The price of freedom

Have you ever thought about how a movement for change comes about? What drives people to get involved? Is there anything that *you* are passionate about? Enough to dedicate your life to?

These are hard questions to answer, but there are – and there always have been – such people. In the next four pages we look at examples of people who have struggled for freedom. As you read the information, think about the following questions:

● What makes people become freedom fighters?
● How important is the role of a leader in struggles for freedom?
● Are there any limits on 'justifiable' action?

What does it take to be a freedom fighter?

> I have always believed that to be a freedom fighter one must suppress many of the personal feelings that makes one feel like a separate individual rather than part of a mass movement. One is fighting for the liberation of millions of people, not the glory of one individual.
>
> Nelson Mandela, *Long Walk to Freedom*, Chapter 11

◀ **Nelson Mandela on his release from prison in 1990**

Freedom fighters sometimes make huge personal sacrifices which can place a heavy burden on their families. Nelson Mandela was unable to watch his children grow up and was not even able to attend the funerals of his eldest son or his mother, both of whom died while he was imprisoned. Similarly, Aung San Suu Kyi has been peacefully campaigning for change in Burma (Myanmar) against an oppressive government which has restricted her political organisation. Her commitment to her cause was so great that when her husband was diagnosed with cancer in England, she refused the offer of a visa to visit him for a final reunion. She feared that she would be blocked from returning to Burma. When her husband died in March 1999 the couple had not seen each other for three years.

▲ **Aung San Suu Kyi, campaigner for democracy in Burma**

People do not begin life as freedom fighters – it is usually a gradual process. Nelson Mandela described it like this:

> I had no epiphany, no singular revelation, no moment of truth, but a steady accumulation of a thousand slights, a thousand indignities, a thousand unremembered moments, produced in me an anger, a rebelliousness, a desire to fight the system which imprisoned my people. There was no particular day on which I said, from henceforth I will devote myself to the liberation of my people; instead, I simply found myself doing so, and could not do otherwise.

Not all freedom fighters live to see their struggle bring about the change they are fighting for. Sometimes, they set the stage for the next generation to achieve their aims.

Tasks

1 Can you think of other people, from history or still living, who have given up parts of their personal and family life to be more effective as a freedom fighter?
2 What would you miss most if you had to give up your personal and family life to fight for a cause?
3 What do you think makes someone become a freedom fighter?
4 What can stop people from taking action?

Freedom fighter, or terrorist?

One of the most difficult issues in international politics is about people who use violence to achieve their political aims. When is this acceptable?

Mandela describes himself as a freedom fighter. In the 1980s Margaret Thatcher, then Prime Minister of Britain, described him as a terrorist.

Is this man a freedom fighter, or a terrorist?

Discussion

Read through the information about South Africa on the next two pages before planning for this discussion.

1 Look at the following definition of terrorism from an American law.
  a Discuss what each point means.
  b Think of real examples you have heard about for each heading. Are they all examples of terrorism?
  c Do you agree with this definition?

'Terrorist activity is any activity which is unlawful under the laws of the place where it is committed (or which, if committed in the USA, would be unlawful) and which involves any of the following:
(i) Hijacking or sabotaging any aircraft, vessel or vehicle.
(ii) Taking hostages to force others (including governments) to undertake specific actions.
(iii) A violent attack on any internationally protected person.
(iv) An assassination.
(v) The use of any:
    (a) biological or chemical agent, or nuclear weapon or device, or
    (b) explosive or firearm (other than for personal monetary gain), with intent to endanger the safety of people or to cause damage to property.
(vi) A threat, attempt, or conspiracy to do any of the above.
(vii) Anyone helping in the planning, funding or other forms of support for terrorism will also be deemed to have engaged in terrorist activity.'

adapted from the Immigration and Nationality Act, USA

2 Take a few minutes to think about the following points, then hold a classroom discussion on the use of violence to achieve political aims.

When, if ever, is it right for political campaigners to use violence?

- Does it matter what campaigning action has been tried already?
- Does it matter what the aims are?
- Does it matter what level of violence is used?
- Does it matter who is targeted?
- Does it matter what the outcome of violence is?
- What might have happened if violence was not used?
- Can governments backed by armies be influenced by violence?
- Is it better to keep the moral high ground and resist others' violence peacefully?
- Does it matter if you live in a democracy?

Discuss your thoughts with the rest of the class.

3 At the end of the discussion, write down your own thoughts and the main reasons for them.

Individual changemakers (2)

Focus on South Africa:
Nelson Mandela and the African National Congress (ANC)

Background

South Africa, like many nations, has a long history of racism, dating back to the arrival of the first European settlers to the continent in the 17th century. Since then and up until the early 1990s, the black majority population were segregated and subjected to many forms of political and economic discrimination. In 1948, when the Nationalist Party came to power, white minority domination in South Africa was officially reinforced. Once in power the new all-white government passed numerous laws to introduce a system of total segregation known as **apartheid**, which means 'apartness' in the Afrikaans language.

The visible signs of apartheid

Fighting apartheid

The ANC, now the majority party in the South African government of National Unity, was founded in 1912. From the beginning it was dedicated to ending racial discrimination. Initially it followed a cautious approach of appealing to Britain to recognise African rights. However, decades of racism and violent attacks on blacks resulted in a more extreme form of African Nationalism. In 1944, Nelson Mandela and other young Nationalists joined together to create what would become an influential wing of the resistance organisation – the ANC Youth League. It quickly found support among the masses.

▲ Nelson Mandela as a young man

The ANC Youth League's programme of activities called for strikes, boycotts and other acts of defiance aimed at ending apartheid. The campaigns of the 1950s marked the beginning of mass resistance to apartheid. Greater numbers of non-black people actively supported the ANC.

March 1960 was a turning point in the history of the fight against apartheid. A huge crowd of 20,000 protesters gathered in a township called Sharpeville. The police responded by opening fire on the unarmed group. During this assault, 69 black people were killed and 186 were injured, the majority of whom were hit in the back.

The Sharpeville massacre, March 1960

The effects of Sharpeville:

- Drew international attention to South Africa's apartheid policy.

- Inspired the world community's gradual isolation of South Africa.

- Marked the end of an era of mainly non-violent resistance to the white majority government.

- The ANC was outlawed and thousands of activists were arrested.

- The ANC went underground and in 1961 took up arms against the government.

- The ANC created a secret military arm – the *Umkhonto we sizwe* ('The Spear of the Nation'), known as MK and headed by Mandela.

In the following 18 months there were over 200 acts of sabotage, including blowing up electricity generators. The government became even more harsh and repressive. In 1962, MK's headquarters were raided and its leaders arrested. At the 1963 Rivonia trial the MK leaders, including Mandela, were charged with high treason – a crime punishable by death. They were convicted and in 1964 were sent to prison where they stayed for 27 years.

Resistance against apartheid continued, led by new activists like Steve Biko. However, in response to and in spite of resistance efforts the apartheid system grew stronger, and its grip was extended over all aspects of life. In 1976, workers' and students' strikes and protest exploded into riots. When the government attempted to force black children in Soweto to learn Afrikaans (a language of white South Africans), tens of thousands of high school students took to the streets. Police opened fire on the marching students, triggering a nationwide uprising that left over a thousand dead.

In the 1980s the government responded with brutality to any resistance, but this did not stop the increasingly restless population demanding civil rights, improved education, universal suffrage and the ending of job limitations, urban segregation and the pass laws. There was also mounting international pressure, including trade sanctions and boycotts.

In 1986, F. W. de Klerk replaced South Africa's long-term President P. W. Botha. De Klerk set about dismantling the structures of apartheid. By 1990 many of the laws of apartheid were being removed, the ANC was legalised, and freedom was granted to political dissidents, including ANC leader Nelson Mandela. In March 1992 white South Africans voted to end apartheid. In 1994 the ANC won a majority in South Africa's first multiracial general election. Along with millions of other black South Africans, Mandela voted for the first time in the election, which chose him as the President of the new democratic South Africa.

> *I have cherished the idea of a democratic and free society in which all persons live together in harmony and with equal opportunity. It is an ideal, which I hope to live for and achieve. But if needs be, it is an ideal for which I am prepared to die.*
>
> from Mandela's speech at his trial, 1964

Tasks

1 What factors helped to end apartheid?

2 Why do you think Nelson Mandela is so widely respected today?

3 What qualities do you think Mandela has that make him a good leader?

4 Think of another leader whom you admire – this could be someone famous, or someone close to home. What qualities do they have that make them a good leader?

Global protestors

Who are they, what do they do and why do they do it?

People all around the world protest about a range of problems, from local unemployment and poverty to global inequality and environmental issues. There is a growing realisation that many of these local and global issues are linked. Protestors often target big business, Western governments, and international organisations such as the World Bank, the World Trade Organisation (WTO) and the International Monetary Fund (IMF). A common complaint is that these organisations put profit before people and promote free trade at the expense of environmental and social considerations.

Most protestors are peaceful but some believe in the use of violence. This minority attacks shops as symbols of big business, and also attacks the police as a symbol of authority. The police have to try to balance the need to keep order with their duty to protect the rights of peaceful protestors to demonstrate and voice their opinions.

If people decide that they do not like the way global organisations and companies work, what can they do to change it? Does protest help? Is there any role for violence?

May Day 2001: London, UK

May Day has become a day known for protest in many countries around the world. Riots broke out in London on May Day in 2000 and police officers and vehicles were attacked. Many protestors and police were concerned that this would be repeated in 2001.

Shaggy, 18, a factory worker

> I'm here to express my opposition to third world poverty and to protest about environmental issues. I'm also giving out peaceful protest leaflets. Of course there are factions that want violence, but I've been very distressed to see the way that the police and the media have concentrated on that.

Ronny, 27, caterer

> I've made veggie burgers to hand out to the Critical Mass cyclists after they've finished their action. I'm involved in campaigning on animal rights.

Tym, 21, works in a toyshop

> I came to the May Day action last year, and I really liked the atmosphere. Everyone was relaxed and it was really chilled out.

adapted from *The Guardian*, 2 May 2001

Force gears up for Mayday mayhem

Officers will not be in riot gear, though batons, shields and other equipment will be carried by mobile units. Some demonstrators are being deterred from joining the protest for fear of arrest, but senior officers still believe that about 800 anarchists will descend on London intent on bloodshed.

adapted from *The Times*, 1 May 2001

What do each of these four photographs say to you about the 2001 May Day protests? Think about how the police and the protestors are shown in each image.

May Day: 6.38pm
Two protestors destroyed CCTV cameras and passed metal bars to protestors trying to smash shop windows. The police mounted a charge on Oxford Street under a hail of bottles.

May Day: 6.50pm
Police hemmed in 1,000 protestors at Oxford Circus and told them to remain calm.

adapted from *The Guardian*, 1 May 2001

February, 1999: India

From the peasant farmers who gathered in huge numbers outside the Karnataka state government offices and laughed all day at their policies, to villagers who swore to drown if their river was dammed, to the fishing unions' strike that involved mass fasting and harbour blockades against industrial overfishing, the protest tactics are as diverse as the movement itself... They are dedicated to non-violent civil disobedience and call for a development based on self-reliance and village-level democracy.

adapted from *The Guardian*, 17 February 1999

July, 2001: New Delhi, India

Nine and a half million central and state government employees have threatened to go on a country-wide strike. The employees would protest against, among other things, downsizing of establishments, abolition of posts and redundancies, changes to existing labour laws, against workers' interests and all other 'disastrous economic policies' being adopted at the dictates of IMF, World Bank and WTO, they said.

adapted from *The Newspaper Today* (www.thenewspapertoday.com)

Tasks

1 What sorts of things make people demonstrate against governments, big business or international organisations?
2 What can people do to show they disagree with these groups?
3 What effect do you think such protests might have?
4 During the 2001 May Day protest Tony Blair, the Prime Minister, said 'there is a right way to protest in a democracy and there is a wrong way'.
   a What do you think he meant by 'a wrong way'?
   b What do you think he meant by 'a right way'?

Class discussion

Some people argue that the media only ever cover violent protests, and this undermines the message of peaceful protestors. Think about the following questions and prepare for a classroom discussion about this issue.

• Why do you think the media show images of violence?
• Would there be so much violence if the media refused to cover it?
• Is police action to control all protestors justified by the actions of the violent minority?
• How would you convince a group not to use violence?

Try to think about what motivates a minority to use violence and how they could be convinced that non-violence is better.

Extension

Other events that have been linked to these protests include:
• the Seattle WTO conference in December 1999
• the Gothenburg EU summit in June 2001
• the Genoa G8 summit in July 2001.

Using the internet, carry out further research on these events and other linked protests around the world. Is there an underlying aim that unites all the protestors, or do they all want separate things? What are the likely results of such protests?

Volunteering

So far we have been looking at ways in which citizens can persuade powerful people and organisations to make decisions in their interest. But there is another important way in which citizens can bring about change – they can do things themselves. Just as campaigns are often more powerful if they involve more people, individual action can also be more effective if it is part of larger organised effort.

Most people have some ideas about what volunteering might be – collecting money on the street, helping in a charity shop or cleaning a canal. It also involves a lot more than this – there is something to suit everybody and there is a lot to be gained.

Fact Box
In the UK:
• There are 185,000 registered charities.
• There are 200,000 voluntary and neighbourhood groups.
• Over 3 million volunteers help in schools, hospitals and social services.
• 23 million people – half the population – do some form of voluntary work.
• There are three groups – the young, the early retired and the retired – who have the most time, but do less volunteering than any other group.

⚠ **What kind of activities do volunteers undertake for these organisations? What other voluntary organisations do you know about?**

Why volunteer?

Volunteering isn't just good for the soul. It can also put you on track to improve your career – and your bank balance.

Whether you're currently studying, in work or out of work, volunteering is a great way to:
● develop new skills
● build your confidence
● show future employees you've got drive and initiative.

These days employers look for more than just qualifications, they're interested in your personal qualities and transferable skills, such as time management and communication. Application forms will ask you to talk about why you're right for the job, based on paid and unpaid employment, so that's the perfect opportunity to make volunteering work for you.

Volunteering can give you a foot in the door you might not otherwise get – the chance to show an employer what you can do, and why they should pay you to do it!

adapted from: **www.do-it.org.uk**

I'm a volunteer organiser for my local Community Service Volunteers. I organise volunteers to go and help out in schools across the borough as well as co-ordinating a group of volunteers who befriend elderly patients at the local hospital. The volunteers visit patients who do not have much support. I was made redundant at 55 because of a heart problem. It would have been difficult to find another job, but rather than sitting in a chair feeling sorry for myself, I decided to help out in my local school, and this developed into running a group of volunteers.

I'd been thinking of doing something for the Terrence Higgins Trust because I have so many friends affected and I'd like to educate myself. While in a gay pub I saw a poster stating, 'Volunteering is for everyone – volunteering is for you'. I was surprised to see a poster that seemed specifically to target the lesbian and gay community – it's nice to get away from the image of the housewife helping Oxfam. I rang the number on the poster and went along to the meeting, I'm currently being trained and am looking forward to the work I will be doing.

After my A levels I had an idea of the direction I wanted to go, but wasn't sure. At a careers fair I spoke to someone from my local volunteer bureau who suggested I volunteer at the local performing arts centre for disabled and able-bodied people. Volunteering gave me the perfect opportunity to think about what I wanted to do, it was great fun and gave me real experience.

After university I wanted to travel and live as part of a different community, before finding a job. I spent a year teaching in a girl's school in Pakistan. I enjoyed the experience and found it challenging to live in such a different culture. People should try to get as much information about the options as possible and really think about what they want to do, and why, before they make their choice.

It pays to volunteer: that's what a group of young people found. Before volunteering, 42% of the 60 participants were unemployed. This figure reduced to 7% after finishing their placement. Sian Austen (27) was unemployed for six months before volunteering. She spent two days a week in a school helping children to read and learn science. She went on to become the paid manager of her local volunteer organisation.

Tasks

1 Look at the examples of why people volunteer (they are based on real people). For each one, say why they became a volunteer.
2 What reasons might people have for *not* volunteering?
3 What would (or did) encourage you to volunteer?

Discussion

Does it matter if people volunteer mainly to improve their own job prospects, or should we volunteer mainly to help other people?

Extension

1 Carry out a survey to find out how many people in your year or school are volunteers. Look at Section 1 'Skills' to help you design an appropriate survey.
2 Working in groups, plan a campaign to recruit more young people to volunteer. Present your campaign strategy to the rest of the class and ask them to assess how effective your campaign is likely to be in achieving its aim.

Individual action for sustainable development

The sustainable family...

... at home
- Solar panels
- Draft strips around doors and windows
- Low-energy light bulbs
- Television, CD player and computer always turned off at the mains
- Dry clothes on washing line whenever possible

... in the garden
- Pond, nesting boxes and bird feeders to encourage wildlife
- Compost pile for kitchen and garden waste
- No chemical sprays
- Collect rainwater in water butts
- Garden table with a Forest Stewardship Council label

... at the shops
- Use local shops and farmers' market to buy locally produced goods in order to cut down on food miles
- Use supermarkets only to buy fair trade coffee, tea and bananas
- Re-use shopping bags
- Try to avoid excess packaging and recycle essential packaging

... travelling around
- Walk or cycle most of the time
- Use the train for longer journeys
- Children walk to school with friends

... in the community
- Use local shops, sports and entertainment facilities
- Get involved in local decision-making
- Be friendly with neighbours, and share tools, swap plant cuttings, babysit and help each other out

... and in the wider world
- Use a bank with an ethical policy
- Buy electricity from a company investing in renewable energy
- Become a member of international organisations that support sustainable development

Tasks

1 Explain how each of the features shown on these pages contributes to sustainable development.
2 Sort the actions of the sustainable family into *social*, *economic* and *environmental* categories (some may fit more than one).
3 List any additional actions the sustainable family could undertake.
4 Do you and your family do any of the things on your list?
5 Compare your answers with those of others in the class – what reasons do people have for doing (or not doing) these things?
6 What would encourage people to do more?

Extension

Choose something that you think would make a difference, and do something about it. Use the active citizenship cycle on pages 12–13 to help you to plan what to do and how to do it. This could be the basis for your coursework.

Further information

For more information and ideas about energy saving at home and school, go to: www.defra.gov.uk and click on Environment.
For further ideas of things we could all do to live more sustainably see: www.doingyourbit.org.uk

Local action for sustainable development

Community action

In many areas, local people join together to improve their environment and quality of life. These groups not only make physical improvements, but also help people to make friends and increase the sense of community. Some groups rely entirely on volunteers while others apply for grant funding from charitable trusts, the local authority or the government. Community groups get involved in many different local issues. They may include:

- support groups for people with particular needs, interests or disabilities
- transport campaign groups, which campaign for better and safer cycling, walking or public transport facilities
- residents' and tenants' associations in which people work together to improve the streets or estates on which they live
- conservation groups which clear ponds and canals or maintain footpaths
- local branches of national or international groups, e.g. Friends of the Earth, which campaign on local environmental issues.

Local Exchange Trading Schemes (LETS)

LETS is one example of an effective community self-help scheme. Local people get together, and compile a directory of skills and goods that they have to offer and need. Someone may, for example, do computer work or lend tools to one person and get lifts, locally grown food, babysitting or haircuts from others. No actual money changes hands. Each member has a personal account which is credited when they do work for people and debited when they use services provided by others.

There are more than 450 LETS schemes in Britain involving over 40,000 people. They give people access to goods and services whether or not they have money to pay for them. It is a great way of meeting new friends and finding a sense of self-worth and belonging, and gives people a chance to develop their skills. Trading goods and services locally reduces transport needs.

Tasks

Carry out a survey of your own local area. Think about the following headings and describe the best and worst area you could imagine for each heading. Add these descriptions to a scale (best to worst). Then add a description of your own local area wherever you think it should fit on the scale. You could write in your facts, draw a sketch or take photographs as evidence.

- Housing
- Shops
- Transport
- Traffic levels
- Noise
- Pollution

- Green spaces
- Things for young people to do
- Level of crime
- Safety

Example for crime:

Worst
Street crime high, mobile-phone theft high, cannot leave things unguarded.

Best
Almost no crime, lockers in school and local pool safe.

My local area
OK as long as you are careful. Very few cases of students thieving from each other.

When you have completed the survey for a variety of headings, list the items for where your area is furthest from the 'best-case' scenario. What local action could be taken by:

a you?
b your school?

c your local authority?
d others?

The role of local authorities

Agenda 21 is an international agreement to work towards sustainable development (meeting human needs without damaging the planet). It states that many of the problems and solutions relating to sustainable development have their roots in local activities. Local authorities are responsible for making decisions about local systems and for implementing national policies. They also have a role in educating and responding to the public to promote sustainable development.

Local Agenda 21

Most local authorities have a 'Local Agenda 21' – a plan for working towards sustainable development in the local area – developed with local groups. Some have developed 'indicators' which they can use to measure whether their efforts are being successful. Look at the following, which are suggested areas for councils to improve. What kinds of *evidence* would help them to judge how successful they had been? The first example has been completed to give you some ideas.

How would you rate your own local area?

MEETING SOCIAL NEEDS

1 Better health and education for all

- Protect human health and well-being through safe, clean, pleasant environments.
- Emphasise health service prevention action as well as care.
- Maximise everyone's access to the skills and knowledge needed for them to play a full part in society.

Evidence
- Death rates and causes
- Qualifications of young people
- Number involved in adult education

2 Access to local services and travel

- Ensure access to good food, water, housing and fuel at a reasonable cost.
- Encourage necessary access to facilities, services, goods and other people in ways that make less use of the car and minimise impacts on the environment.
- Make opportunities for culture, leisure and recreation readily available to all.
- Meet needs locally wherever possible.

3 Shaping our surroundings

- Create or improve places, spaces and buildings that work well, wear well and look well.
- Make settlements 'human' in scale and form.
- Value and protect diversity and local distinctiveness and strengthen local community and cultural identity.

4 Empowerment and participation

- Empower all sections of the community to participate in decision-making and consider the social and community impacts of decisions.

Tasks

1 Do you agree with the choice of targets? Would you change or add any?
2 According to the evidence requirements you have drawn up, how is your own local area doing?
3 The list on the left relates to social issues. What do you think your local authority should include in its targets for the local environment and for the local economy?
4 What would your top priorities be for your local authority?
5 What action is your local authority taking to encourage sustainable development?

Further information

See: **www.sustainable-development.gov.uk** for more information on a sustainable society.
For examples of the different ways that some areas are tackling LA21 issues, see: **www.ealing.gov.uk** and search for Local Agenda 21, or **www.northsomerset-la21.org.uk** or go to: **www.carrick.gov.uk** and search for Local Agenda 21.

National action for sustainable development

The UK strategy

As part of the Agenda 21 international agreement, the UK government has devised a *National Strategy for Sustainable Development* in order to explain the process through which it will work towards improving quality of life for people now, without damaging the planet for the future.

The *Strategy* is called 'A better quality of life', and it has four main aims:
- social progress that recognises the needs of everyone
- effective protection of the environment
- responsible use of natural resources
- high levels of economic growth and employment.

The government has broken down each aim into a series of objectives and 'indicators' so that progress can be measured.

SOURCE A

Some of the government targets from 'A better quality of life'

Effective protection of the environment	
Objectives	**Indicators**
• Continue to reduce our emissions (of greenhouse gases) now, and plan for greater reductions in the longer term	Emissions of greenhouse gases
• Reduce air pollution and ensure that air quality continues to improve through the longer term	Days when air pollution is moderate or high
• Reduce the need to travel and improve choice in transport	Road traffic
• Improve river quality	Rivers of good or fair quality
• Reverse the long-term decline in populations of farmland and woodland birds	Populations of wild birds
• Re-use previously developed land, in order to protect the countryside and encourage urban regeneration	New homes built on previously developed land

The government has set up a Sustainable Development Commission, whose members are independent of government, to recommend action and to monitor progress.

SOURCE B

Government progress

In 2002, the government report showed some progress:

✔ Economic output – 8% growth in GDP

✔ Children in poverty – 34% to 32%

✔ Air quality – number of days with moderate or high pollution down from 40 to 16 per year

✘ Violent crime – increased by 20%

adapted from 2002 Government Report 'Achieving a better quality of life' Chapter 3

SOURCE C

The patient still needs urgent treatment, says Friends of the Earth

Charles Secrett, director:

❝ Whilst some indicators show some welcome improvements, there are still areas for serious concern. Traffic levels are still rising, the huge mountains of waste we create are growing larger, and wildlife is under pressure. These trends must be reversed. ❞

Friends of the Earth is calling for changes in the next Budget including:
- the re-introduction of the fuel price escalator
- the introduction of a pesticide tax.

adapted from FoE press release, 14 March 2002

Government Action 1: Taxation

In order to achieve environmental objectives, the government has to find ways to persuade businesses and individuals to make changes. One way is to increase taxes on activities they want to discourage. An example of this was the Fuel Tax Escalator, introduced by the Conservative government and continued by Labour, which increased petrol taxes every year. The reason given was that it would protect the environment by persuading people to use their cars less.

In the summer of 2000, angry at the increasing cost of petrol, lorry drivers around the country blockaded oil refineries and tried to persuade motorists not to buy petrol. This campaign had the opposite effect, as people stockpiled petrol for fear of shortages.

One objection to the Fuel Tax Escalator was that the money raised was not spent on public transport or researching more environmentally friendly forms of energy. The Treasury has now scrapped the Escalator and has agreed to use any future petrol tax rises to improve public transport and the road network. However, the increasing price of petrol (70% of which is taxes) may have contributed to the development of more fuel-efficient cars.

Fuel protestors blockade Panic petrol buying

△ **Why did protestors take such action? What else can the government do to cut traffic levels?**

Government Action 2: Legislation

Members of Parliament can also encourage people to do things that will help to achieve environmental objectives. The Home Energy Conservation Act was introduced as a Private Members' Bill by a Liberal Democrat MP and, with the support of government, became law in 1995. It requires all UK local authorities to identify energy-saving measures that would be cost-effective and likely to increase energy efficiency in all homes in their area.

Government Action 3: Education

A section in Agenda 21 commits the governments that signed it to 'Reorienting education towards sustainable development'. Organisations promoting environment and development education saw this as an opportunity to get such issues into the centre of the education system, and lobbied government to take action. The government set up a Panel for Education for Sustainable Development in England which included representatives from the Royal Society for the Protection of Birds, the Development Education Association, B&Q, the World Wide Fund for Nature (WWF) and Forum for the Future, as well as from exam boards and teaching associations.

The Panel wrote a report on 'Education for Sustainable Development' (ESD) to contribute to the National Curriculum Review for 2000. Educating pupils for sustainable development is now part of the stated aims of the curriculum and should be taught in a range of subjects. The National Curricula for Scotland, Wales and Northern Ireland are organised differently, but all include sustainable development education.

Tasks

1 The National Curriculum should develop your 'awareness and understanding of, and respect for, the environments in which you live, and secure your commitment to sustainable development at a personal, local, national and global level' (from the National Curriculum for England, 'Values, aims and purposes').
  a Do you think this is happening in your school?
  b Which subjects and topics do you think contribute to this?
  c What could you do to contribute to this aim in your school?

2 Do you think government is doing enough to promote sustainable development?
3 Which do you think is more important in promoting sustainable development?
  a The actions of individuals and their families
  b Local authorities
  c Central government
  d Charities and other non-governmental organisations
4 Look at sources B and C and the photograph. What factors does government have to think about before introducing changes to taxation?

International action for sustainable development

International conferences

In 1992, leaders from more than 150 countries around the world met in Rio at the United Nations Conference on Environment and Development, the 'Earth Summit'. They were concerned that human activity was damaging the planet and putting life in the future at risk. They began to plan for sustainable development – ways to meet human needs and improve quality of life without damaging the planet.

A number of international agreements resulted from this conference, including:

- *Agenda 21*, a plan to work towards sustainable development in the 21st century
- the *Convention on Climate Change*, the aim of which was to stabilise emissions of greenhouse gases
- the *Convention on Biological Diversity*, designed to conserve biodiversity internationally.

The Commission on Sustainable Development was set up to monitor and encourage the development and implementation of these agreements. There have been several more conferences since Rio to try to set legally binding targets and timescales to the agreements.

A second World Summit on Sustainable Development was held in Johannesburg in 2002. It brought together tens of thousands of participants, including heads of state and government, national delegates from non-governmental organisations (NGOs), and representatives of business and industry, of children and youth groups, farmers, indigenous people, local authorities, scientific and technological communities, women and workers and trade unions.

They considered progress in the ten years since the Rio summit, asking questions such as: 'Has global poverty got worse or better?' 'Are we consuming too much of the Earth's precious resources?' 'What impact has human activity had on the air we breathe, on our fresh water, and on the world's oceans and forests?' They looked at the record of the participating countries in implementing the agreements made at Rio, and recommended further action.

▲ The 1992 Rio conference in session

▲ Protestors at the Rio summit

Discussion

- How useful are international conferences?
- Is it possible to reach meaningful agreements between hundreds of countries?
- How can people be held to their promises?

The European Union

In May 2001 the EU agreed a *European Strategy for Sustainable Development*, which identifies unsustainable trends such as global warming and transport congestion, and suggests that all new policies should have sustainable development as their core concern.

In February 2002, the European Parliament voted by 540 to 4 to accept the Kyoto Agreement, which binds Europe to an 8% cut in carbon dioxide emissions by 2010. The USA (with only 4% of the world's population and producing 25% of all carbon dioxide emissions) refused to sign for fear that it would limit economic growth. The EU only sees 8% as a start and further aims to reduce greenhouse gas emissions by an average of 1% per year up to 2020.

Discussion

- What point is there in the EU acting if the USA does not?

Non-governmental organisations (NGOs)

Some NGOs are international, with branches in many countries, and are concerned with issues of sustainable development such as social justice, improving quality of life, and environmental conservation. They run publicity campaigns to raise public awareness, and lobby governments and companies to encourage them to take such issues into account. They often have specialist knowledge about particular issues, and can offer advice at all levels, from members of the public to governments and the United Nations.

For example, the World Wide Fund for Nature (WWF) campaigns to raise public awareness of environmental issues and sustainability, and protects threatened wildlife. It does this by selling fair trade and environmentally friendly goods, collecting donations and working with local organisations to protect the habitat of animals whilst helping local people make money.

Discussion

- What other NGOs do you know about that are involved in promoting sustainable development?
- What do they do to support their aims?

The media

In preparation for the Johannesburg World Summit on Sustainable Development, journalists from South Africa, China, Brazil, the UK and the USA met to discuss the role of the media regarding sustainable development. They agreed that the media has the power to influence how people and politicians think and act. However, all the journalists present talked about the difficulty of getting reports about sustainable development broadcast. One said that environmental and development issues were not usually considered headline news – they might get air time on quiet days but not on days when there was a lot of news.

Another journalist said she had begun to focus on people involved with the issues, whom the audience could relate to and care about. In Brazil, they had found that environmental campaigns, and inserting environmental issues into soap operas, were successful ways of raising public interest and awareness.

Discussion

- If the media is so powerful, why do journalists feel they cannot publicise sustainable development issues?
- Do you think viewers would just turn over channels?

Tasks

1 Make a list of issues connected with sustainable development that you think affect the whole world and not just one country.
2 Do you think enough is happening to solve these problems?
3 What additional action do you think needs to be agreed at a global level?

Summary

Look back over the last eight pages.
1 Write down your own definition of **sustainable development**.
2 Try to answer the following questions as honestly as you can. In relation to sustainable development:
 a What *could* you do?
 b What *should* you do?
 c What *will* you do?
3 What should others do? Specify who and what.

Further information

For further information about sustainable development and the international summits, see:
www.earthsummit2002.org and
www.johannesburgsummit.org

Revision

Now that you have worked through Section 4, you should be able to answer the following short-answer questions. Once you have worked through the questions, check your answers with others in the class and with your teacher, and use the facts to start a set of revision cards. These can be completed as you work through other topic areas in your Citizenship Studies course.

A   Short answers

1   When did women get the vote in Britain?
2   List **two** groups who cannot vote.
3   What is the **electoral register**?
4   Name **three** political parties.
5   What electoral system is used to select MPs for Westminster?
6   Name **one** other type of electoral system.
7   What is a **constituency**?
8   Why is a **secret ballot** used in elections?
9   What is **tactical voting**?
10   List **three** possible reasons for low voter turnout.
11   List **three** possible solutions to the problem of low turnout.
12   Describe **one** way in which the internet can be used to encourage people to get involved in campaigning.
13   Give **one** reason why people volunteer.
14   Give **one** reason why some people do not volunteer.
15   What is **sustainable development**?
16   List **three** ways in which individuals can promote sustainable development.
17   List **three** ways in which local government can promote sustainable development.
18   List **three** ways in which central government can promote sustainable development.
19   Name **one** international charity.
20   List **three** things your named charity does to achieve its aims.

B Source-based questions

SOURCE A

'I'm not interested in the bloody system! Why has he no food? Why is he starving to death?'

Bob Geldof

SOURCE B

'When I give food to the poor, they call me a saint. When I ask why the poor have no food, they call me a communist.'

Dom Helder Camara

1 What similarities are there between these two quotations?

2 Why do you think giving to charity is not always enough to solve a problem?

3 What else can you do to help other people?

C Extended answers

Write an essay on **one** of the following topics. Remember to use evidence, and consider the issue from different viewpoints. You may express your own opinion in the conclusion.

1 'Voting is the most important way in which we can achieve change.' Do you agree?

- In what ways does voting create change?
- Is it equally important for everyone?
- What other methods can citizens use?
- Is voting enough to be an active citizen?

2 How can UK citizens influence global issues?

- Individual action
- Issues
- Organisations
- Government

3 'People should just look out for themselves and their families and not worry about what everyone else is up to.' Do you agree?

- Arguments for this point of view
- Arguments against this point of view
- Effects of such a policy

D Active ideas

You may choose to become involved in active experience relating to elections and campaigning. The following are some ideas.

1 Help to run an election in the school.

2 Start a campaign in your own school about any issue of interest and importance.

3 Work with other students or your school council to plan campaign strategies.

4 Establish a school branch of a campaigning organisation, such as Amnesty.

5 Form an action group to help your school become more sustainable.

Agenda 21 An international agreement between governments to promote sustainable development and tackle global warming.

apartheid Racist political, social and economic system that existed in South Africa to treat people differently on the basis of their skin colour.

asylum-seeker A person who has left their own country and is applying for refugee status in another country.

barrister A lawyer who is able to present a case in court.

budget Every year the Chancellor of the Exchequer sets a budget which describes the ways in which the government will collect and spend money.

Cabinet The group of politicians with responsibility for making government decisions. In central government the Cabinet includes Secretaries of State and senior Ministers. In local government, members of the Cabinet have responsibility for one of the councils activities.

campaign A co-ordinated attempt to put across an opinion or point of view to others. Political parties campaign to get their candidates elected; community and voluntary groups often campaign to raise awareness of their particular area of concern.

candidate A person who stands in an election and for whom people can vote to be their representative.

Civil Law Deals with laws that are concerned with relationships between individual citizens and organisations, e.g. family law.

Civil Service The group of workers who put government policy into practice.

Commonwealth A particular group of countries whose governments occasionally meet to co-operate on a range of issues. Most of the Commonwealth member states were part of the former British Empire.

community A group of people who share interests and values. The term often applies to people who also live close together.

constituency In the UK, the area represented by a Member of Parliament.

consumer rights The rights and legal protection available to people when they buy goods or services.

convention An international agreement between states in which governments agree to pursue the same goals; for example, the *Convention on the Rights of the Child* sets out the rights that governments agree to protect and respect.

Criminal Law Deals with laws the state has established to protect individuals and society from harm, e.g. murder and theft.

Crown Court The court where the most serious criminal cases are tried in front of a judge and often a jury.

Crown Prosecution Service (CPS) The government service that decides who will be taken to court, based on the evidence available.

devolution The process of moving power from central government to regional and local government.

discrimination Unfair treatment of individuals or groups based on aspects of their identity or background, e.g. ethnicity, gender, disability, sexuality, religion, marital status.

electoral register The list of names and addresses of all the people who can vote. Citizens must register their details if they want to vote.

equal opportunities Policies and laws that seek to ensure that discrimination does not take place and that everyone has the same chances of success regardless of differences in ethnicity, gender, age, disability, etc.

EU (European Union) A group of states that have joined together to co-operate on a number of issues, such as trade and farming.

Euro The single currency adopted by most countries in the EU.

'first past the post' Electoral system in which each voter has one choice and the candidate with biggest share of the vote wins the election.

free speech The right to free speech is important in democracies; it enables people to make their own opinions public and to criticise the government.

GDP (Gross Domestic Product) The total measure of goods and services produced in a country by its population. GDP is used as a measure of the wealth of countries.

general election The national election for Members of Parliament which in the UK must happen at least every five years.

House of Commons The more powerful of the two Houses of Parliament. Members are directly elected by voters in constituencies.

House of Lords Members of the House of Lords are not elected; they work mainly to check and revise proposed laws as they go through Parliament. The House of Commons can reject their proposals if they disagree. The Lords is also the highest court in the country — cases are decided by a small group of senior lawyers called the Law Lords.

Human Rights Act A law establishing the rights of individuals which the government should respect in all its work.

indirect discrimination Action that may have the unintended effect of discriminating against a group; for example, a height limit of ë6 feetí would discriminate against women who are on average shorter than men.

judge Senior lawyer who makes decisions on questions of law in court (but not in a Magistratesí Court) and who passes an appropriate sentence when someone are convicted.

jury Twelve ordinary citizens who are randomly selected to hear cases in a Crown Court. Their task is to weigh up the evidence and decide if the accused person is guilty or innocent.

lobbying Attempts to convince politicians to support oneís own view.

Local Agenda 21 Local government plans and policies to promote sustainable development and tackle global warming.

Magistrates' Court Most court appearances take place in these courts. There is no jury or judge — instead members of the local community, who give their time as magistrates, weigh-up the evidence and decide on guilt or innocence.

manifesto The document prepared by a political party before an election, detailing what actions the party would take if it was elected.

monarchy The king or queen as head of state.

MP (Member of Parliament) Elected representative in the House of Commons.

Northern Ireland Assembly The elected government for Northern Ireland. Some powers were devolved from the UK government to the Assembly.

opposition Political parties that are not part of the government. The official opposition is the second largest party in the House of Commons.

Parliament The institution that passes laws.

political party An organisation that has a range of aims and objectives and puts forward candidates in elections.

pressure group An organisation that has a specific set of aims and puts pressure on politicians and other decision-makers to achieve its goals.

Prime Minister The leader of the government.

proportional representation Any electoral system that tries to reflect the proportion of support for parties in the number of representatives elected.

refugee A person who has fled their own country, owing to a well-founded fear of persecution there, in order to seek safety in another country.

Scottish Parliament The elected government for Scotland. Some powers were devolved from the UK government to the Scottish Parliament.

sustainable development Development that does not damage the environment and does not use resources that will threaten life in the future.

United Nations International organisation that seeks to promote peace and friendly relations between nations.

volunteer Someone who gives up their time to work for no wage.

Welsh Assembly The elected government for Wales. Some powers were devolved from the UK government to the Assembly.